THE OLDWAYS 4-WEEK

MEDITERRANEAN DIET MENU PLAN

For anyone who loves food, the flavors of tradition are too delicious, too meaningful, and ultimately, too important to give up. No organization understands this better than Oldways. It was Oldways that, in conjunction with some of the world's top nutritionists and scientists, came up with the innovative Mediterranean Diet Pyramid.

— *Cooking Light*

rediscover goodness

OLDWAYS

CULTURAL FOOD TRADITIONS

Oldways is a nonprofit dedicated to improving public health by inspiring individuals and organizations to embrace the healthy, sustainable joys of the "old ways" of eating—heritage-based diets high in taste, nourishment, sustainability, and joy. Oldways created the original Mediterranean Diet Pyramid in 1993. Since then, we have worked tirelessly to spread the word about this healthy and delicious way of eating.

Inspired by the popularity of our original Oldways 4-Week Mediterranean Diet Menu Plan, we are pleased to announce the release of this new edition, featuring the best guidance, recipes, and meal planning tips of our original book, along with 40 NEW recipes, and a sleek new look.

This book is dedicated to the late K. Dun Gifford, founder of Oldways, who partnered with scientists, food and wine producers, policymakers, and chefs around the globe to document and celebrate the joys and benefits of the Mediterranean Diet.

You can learn more about Oldways at OldwaysPT.org

We want to thank the members of the Mediterranean Foods Alliance for their generous support in helping us promote the remarkable health benefits of the Mediterranean Diet.

For information about special discounts for bulk purchases,
or about co-branding options, please contact Oldways:
1-617-421-5500 or store@OldwaysPT.org.

ISBN 978-0-9858939-5-8

Every effort has been made to ensure that the information in this book is complete and accurate. However, this book is not intended as a substitute for consulting with your physician. All matters regarding your health require medical supervision. The authors will not be liable for any loss or damage allegedly arising from any information or suggestion in this book.

INTRODUCTION

Welcome to the Mediterranean Diet   4

The Mediterranean Diet Pyramid   5

8 Simple Steps   6

Get Ready, Get Set, Cook   8

    Cooking Basics   8

    Equipment You'll Need   8

    Stocking Your Pantry   9

OLDWAYS 4-WEEK MENU PLAN

Menu Tips and Tricks   10

Substitute Ingredients   12

Breakfast 1-2-3 Plan   13

Lunch Ideas   14

Daily Menus and Recipes   16-79

    Week 1   16

    Week 2   32

    Week 3   48

    Week 4   64

BONUS PAGES

Day 29+   80

Tips for Healthier Eating   81

Mediterranean Desserts   82

Dressing Basics   86

A Guide to Whole Grains   88

    Grain Cooking Chart   90

Snacks at a Glance   92

Recipe Index and Nutritionals   96

Index   98

WELCOME TO THE MEDITERRANEAN DIET

The Mediterranean Diet is not a diet, as in "go on a diet," even though it's a great way to lose weight and improve your health. Rather, it's a lifestyle, based upon the traditional foods (and drinks) of the countries that surround the Mediterranean Sea. Scores of leading scientists have rated this way of eating as one of the healthiest diets in the world— while millions of people like you have rated it one of the most delicious!

The Mediterranean Diet is all about cooking and eating simple, wholesome, minimally-processed foods, being active, enjoying delicious meals with friends and family, and (if you choose) drinking wine in moderation with those meals.

Best of all, you don't need to travel any further than your local supermarket to find all the ingredients you need. It's so easy and affordable to bring the remarkable Mediterranean style of eating to your own kitchen.

Once you make a few simple but profound changes in the way you eat today, you'll see how rewarding (and delicious) it is to follow this traditional eating pattern for the rest of your life.

All of these meals—and more—are part of the Mediterranean Diet, a way of eating with so many options that you'll happily eat this way from now on.

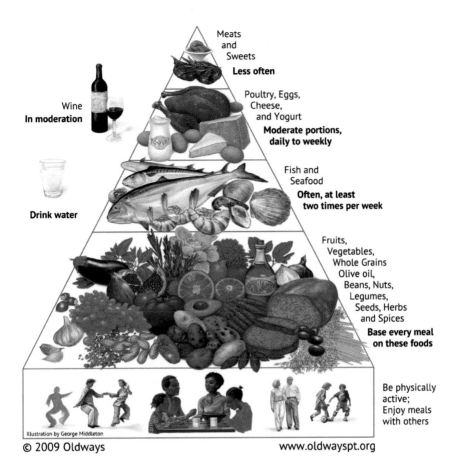

Meats
and
Sweets
Less often

Poultry, Eggs,
Cheese,
and Yogurt
**Moderate portions,
daily to weekly**

Wine
In moderation

Fish and
Seafood
**Often, at least
two times per week**

Drink water

Fruits,
Vegetables,
Whole Grains
Olive oil,
Beans, Nuts,
Legumes,
Seeds, Herbs
and Spices
**Base every meal
on these foods**

Be physically
active;
Enjoy meals
with others

Illustration by George Middleton

© 2009 Oldways   www.oldwayspt.org

MEDITERRANEAN DIET PYRAMID

The Mediterranean Diet Pyramid is your guide to good food from the bottom (most important!) on up. Since the rest of this book focuses on food, we'd like to draw attention to the lifestyle activities that make up the base of the pyramid.

Look for ways to be more active. Good food alone isn't enough to live a healthy life.

Cooking and enjoying the pleasures of the table with family and friends contribute hugely to good health.

8 SIMPLE STEPS

MEDITERRANEAN SECRETS FOR GOOD HEALTH

It's easy to bring the remarkable health benefits and affordable Mediterranean style of eating to your kitchen cupboards, your refrigerator, your counter tops, your stovetop, your oven, and your table every day.

The menus you'll find in this book are built upon these 8 simple steps:

1. Eat lots of vegetables.

There are so many choices! From a simple plate of sliced fresh tomatoes drizzled with olive oil and topped with crumbled feta cheese to stunning salads, garlicky greens, fragrant soups and stews, healthy pizzas, or oven-roasted medleys, vegetables are vitally important to the fresh tastes and delicious flavors of the Mediterranean Diet. With mixed dishes typical of the Mediterranean, it is even easier to make half of your plate (or bowl) vegetables. Choose recipes like grain bowls, vegetable-based soups, and salads as a delicious strategy to incorporate more produce into your daily routine.

2. Change the way you think about meat.

If you eat meat, have smaller amounts. For example, add small strips of sirloin to a vegetable sauté, or garnish a dish of pasta with diced prosciutto. As a main course, have smaller portions (3 ounces or less) of chicken or lean meat.

3. Include some dairy products.

Choose plain Greek yogurt and smaller amounts of a variety of traditional, artisan cheeses.

4. Eat seafood twice a week.

Fish such as tuna, herring, salmon, and sardines are rich in heart-healthy omega-3 fatty acids, and shellfish including mussels, oysters, and clams have similar benefits for brain and heart health.

5. Cook a vegetarian meal at least one night a week.

Build these meals around beans, whole grains, and vegetables; heighten the flavor with fragrant herbs and spices. When one night feels comfortable, try two nights per week.

6. Use good fats.

Include sources of healthy fats in daily meals, especially extra-virgin olive oil, nuts, peanuts, sunflower seeds, olives, and avocados.

7. Switch to whole grains.

Whole grains are healthier, with more fiber, more protein, and higher levels of many essential nutrients than their refined counterparts. Cook traditional Mediterranean grains like bulgur, freekeh, barley, farro, and brown rice. Favor products made with whole grain flour. Even those on gluten-free diets can benefit from switching to whole grains like brown rice, quinoa, or sorghum. After all, gluten-free does not mean grain-free.

8. For dessert, eat fresh fruit.

Choose from a wide range of delicious fruits—from fresh figs and oranges to pomegranates, grapes, and apples. Dried fruits such as raisins, prunes, dried apricots, and dried cherries are also very Mediterranean. Instead of daily ice cream or cookies, save sweets for a special treat or celebration. In this menu book, we offer one celebration dessert each week, while fresh fruit is the typical daily dessert.

GET READY, GET SET, COOK

The best way to eat healthy, affordable food is to prepare it or assemble it yourself from good ingredients. If you're already comfortable cooking, that's great. If you're not in the habit of cooking, these two pages will tell you the essentials you need to know to make the simple dishes in our Mediterranean Diet plan.

COOKING BASICS

Exact measurements aren't usually important, unless you're baking. If our recipes say "1 (14.5-ounce) can of tomatoes," don't worry if your can is a little bigger or a little smaller. There are three main ways to cook food in your kitchen: in a lot of liquid or a little oil on the stovetop, or roasting/grilling/baking in the oven.

To cook food in water (or broth), turn the burner on high until the water bubbles rapidly (boils), then turn it down until the water barely bubbles (simmers), and cook according to directions.

To cook food in oil, heat a small amount of oil in a pan. Never let it smoke; that means it's too hot. Stir the food around in the oil frequently (sauté). Cook according to directions.

To cook food in the oven, see recipe directions.

EQUIPMENT YOU'LL NEED

You don't need a lot of fancy gadgets to cook the meals in this book. You'll be fine if you have the following:

a large skillet (fry pan)	a cutting board
a few sauce pans with covers	a can opener
a large stock pot or soup kettle	a few mixing bowls
a measuring cup	a colander or strainer
measuring spoons	a large mixing spoon
a sharp knife	dish towel(s)
a vegetable peeler	pot holder(s)
a grater	a food processor or blender

STOCKING YOUR PANTRY

Cooking is easier when you have basic ingredients on hand in your kitchen cabinets, refrigerator, or freezer. Most of the basics on this list keep for a long time, so you buy everything once, then just replace as needed:

SEASONINGS
salt
pepper
oregano
cinnamon
cumin
curry powder
garlic cloves
ginger
sugar
honey
vinegar

IN THE FREEZER
frozen shrimp
frozen berries
frozen veggies

OILS
extra-virgin olive oil

CANS, JARS, AND BOXES
low-sodium black beans
low-sodium white beans
	(e.g. cannellini, navy)
chickpeas
dried lentils
low-sodium broth
oatmeal
bulgur
brown rice
pasta
diced tomatoes
tuna
nuts and peanuts
seeds (sunflower, pumpkin, etc.)
dried fruit

Keep a List on the Refrigerator

When anything runs low, jot it down on the list. About once a week, buy replacements, perishable foods, and special ingredients for specific recipes, such as:

fresh fruits
fresh vegetables
chicken, fish or meat
eggs

cheese
yogurt
whole grain bread and rolls

MENU TIPS AND TRICKS

The menus you'll find on the following pages are designed to take you on a 28-day journey through many of the delicious and satisfying tastes of the Mediterranean Diet. Unlike most diets, the Mediterranean Diet doesn't cut out all the good stuff and leave you feeling deprived. Because it features a wide variety of foods that are just naturally healthier and lower in calories, you'll find you can enjoy "good taste" and "good for you" at the same time.

HOW TO USE THESE MENUS

Feel free to mix and match, taking a breakfast from one day, lunch from another, and dinner or dessert from a third day. You may find one breakfast you especially like and eat it day after day, or pick seven dinners you want to cook week after week. Follow your taste buds—this is not a rigid plan!

The plan starts with ideas for breakfasts and lunches designed to fit your busy schedule and follows with a day-by-day set of menus that mix these breakfasts and lunches with inspiring but easy-to-cook dinners.

Each recipe has fewer than 500 calories. For most people, this level will constitute a weight-loss diet. Once you've achieved your weight goal, check out our "Extras" in the Bonus Pages section for snacks and additions you may enjoy.

We have not included "nutritionals" detailing the calories, fat, sodium, etc. for each day. All our recipes are healthy, and when you eat plenty of fresh vegetables, fruits, and whole grains in reasonable portion sizes, you don't need to obsess about numbers. How much more enjoyable to focus on the tastes of your meal than on the calories and grams of this or that! However, we've included nutritional analyses in our Recipe Index (page 96) for health professionals or others who may need them.

Grain and Vegetable Sides

Many of our menu plans suggest a grain pairing, such as brown rice or farro. Generally, ½ cup cooked whole grains is considered one serving of grains in the Dietary Guidelines for Americans.

Many of our menu plans also suggest a vegetable pairing, such as sautéed kale or roasted carrots. Vegetables are a vital part of the Mediterranean Diet, and the Dietary Guidelines for Americans recommend that most adults get 2 or 3 cups of vegetables daily. However, these menu plans are intended to be used as a guide, and we welcome you to adjust the grain and vegetable servings to meet your dietary needs.

Beverage Suggestions

We have not included beverages in this menu plan. Feel free to enjoy a cup or two of tea or coffee daily, with or without a splash of milk. For most meals, water is the drink of choice. For those who choose to drink alcohol, wine can be part of meal times and social gatherings in moderation (meaning up to one 5-ounce glass of wine per day for women, or up to two glasses for men). After all, wine has historically been an important part of religious rituals, social relationships, and celebrations in the Mediterranean.

Grain Leftovers

Many whole grains in the menu plan can be repurposed throughout the week. For example, the farro on Day 1 can also be reheated for dinner on Day 3. Feel free to cook extra whole grains at the beginning of the week to streamline your dinner prep.

Here's another idea: if you have extra grains left over from dinner, warm them up with a little milk, cinnamon, honey, and fruit. You'll find it makes an unexpectedly delicious and satisfying breakfast.

Weekend Breakfasts

For weekends (or days when you're not so rushed), we've included suggestions that are a bit more elaborate, such as one of these choices:

Eggs Shakshouka (Day 24)

Veggie Omelet (Day 27)

Remember, breakfast doesn't have to be limited to traditional breakfast foods. If you want to warm up some soup or enjoy a big plate of roasted vegetables for breakfast, be our guest!

SUBSTITUTE INGREDIENTS

We've included a range of typically Mediterranean ingredients in our menus so that you can explore some new tastes. However, we realize some of these ingredients may not be available in your store or may cost more than other choices.

ORIGINAL INGREDIENT	PERFECTLY GOOD SUBSTITUTE
Arugula	Baby spinach, any leaf lettuce
Brie or goat cheese	Any spreadable soft cheese
Butternut squash	Sweet potato, or other winter squash (like acorn or delicata)
Cannellini beans	Navy beans, chickpeas, lentils
Fennel bulb	Celery
Feta cheese	Parmesan cheese
Farfalle, Penne, Rotini, Ziti, Shells	Any shaped pasta
Herbs, fresh	Dried herbs (⅓ of original amount)
Kasseri cheese	Provolone cheese (or Swiss cheese)
Linguine	Any long thin pasta
Manchego cheese	Parmigiano-Reggiano, Pecorino Romano, sharp cheddar, or any hard, salty cheese
Olives, Greek, Kalamata, or black	Any olives
Pecorino Romano cheese	Parmigiano-Reggiano, sharp cheddar, or any hard, salty cheese
Whole wheat orzo	Any cooked whole grain
Zucchini	Any other summer squash

Although our recipes may be subtly different with these substitutes, they'll still be delicious.

BREAKFAST ❶ ❷ ❸ PLAN

A HEALTHY START

Eating breakfast starts the day off right. A good breakfast includes whole grains and fruit, along with eggs, milk, yogurt, or some other source of protein. Use this 1-2-3 plan to build your own healthy breakfast. **Choose one item from each category (1-2-3) every day.** Coffee, tea, or water top off the meal.

For your whole grains, pick one bread and one spread:

Bread (1-2 ounces)	**Spread (1-2 tablespoons)**
Whole grain toast	Peanut (or any nut) butter
Whole grain bagel	Hummus
Whole grain pita	Soft cheese
Whole grain English muffin	Avocado

Or, **eat cereal.** Enjoy your whole grains in the form of oatmeal or your favorite cold whole grain cereal, about ½ to 1 cup, with about the same amount of milk, yogurt, or soy or nut milk.

❶

Pick your favorite fruit—**a small to medium whole fruit, about ½ to 1 cup cut-up fruit, or about ¼ cup dried fruit.** Actual fruit will satisfy you better than fruit juice. Pick your favorites according to the season!

Apples	Cherries	Kiwifruit	Peaches
Bananas	Figs	Melon	Pears
Berries	Grapes	Oranges	

❷

Add an egg, yogurt, or a handful of nuts to help your breakfast stick with you until lunch time. Some quick ideas:

Walnuts, almonds, or other nuts—as many as can fit in your cupped hand

Yogurt—buy plain Greek or regular, and add your own fruit or flavorings

Hard-boiled eggs—make several ahead to last the week

Low-fat milk, or soy or nut milk—on its own, or with your cereal

Soft-cooked or scrambled egg—surprisingly quick

❸

LUNCH IDEAS

For lunch, most of our menus feature leftovers and three Mediterranean standbys: salads, wraps or stuffed pitas, and soups.

SALADS

You've got a treat in store as you explore the universe of Mediterranean-style salads!

Green Salads

Green salads feature leafy greens like arugula, spinach, and mixed greens, but you can substitute whatever is available. Romaine is good, for instance. Add a few chopped vegetables and some nuts, peanuts, or seeds and toss with a delicious vinaigrette.

Grain Salads

Mix a half-cup of leftover cooked whole grains—any variety—with your favorite chopped vegetables or leftover roasted vegetables, then toss with a light vinaigrette. Grain salads are great for lunch at work because they don't get soggy before noon.

Pasta Salads

Leftover pasta can also serve as the base for a quick salad. It's especially tasty mixed with chopped vegetables, greens, canned tuna, and an herb vinaigrette.

Nuts, peanuts, seeds (sunflower, pumpkin, etc.), and beans add flavor accents and stick-with-you protein to your favorite salads.

WRAPS OR STUFFED PITAS

Wraps can be made with any kind of whole grain flat bread, including lavaash and tortillas. A round of whole grain pita bread cut in half makes the perfect pocket to hold just about any filling. Some ideas you'll find in our menus include:

Meze Rollup (Day 6)

Sundried Tomato Pesto and White Bean Wrap (Day 26)

SOUPS

Home-made soups offer more taste and less sodium than store-bought ones. Make a batch on the weekend and freeze in single-serving portions. Before long you'll have a "soup factory" in your freezer: just grab a container as you head out the door and warm your soup up in the microwave at work. Some of the soup recipes we've included here are:

Lentil Soup (Day 3)

Minestrone (Day 7)

Hearty Tomato Soup with Citrus Cod (Day 9)

Moroccan Spiced Carrot Soup (Day 25)

YOUR OWN MEZE PLATE AT WORK

In Eastern Mediterranean countries, people often enjoy a meze plate—a collection of small bites. If you have a breakroom fridge at work, stock it with a container of olives, some hummus, and some cheese to make your own **Meze Plate** (Day 5) for lunch. For a Spanish-inspired version, try our **Spanish Picnic** (Day 14).

ENJOY LEFTOVERS

Most of our recipes make enough for four people. If you don't have four people in your household, then you'll have leftovers you can take to work the next day for lunch or reheat for another dinner. If you think you'll have no leftovers, double your dinner recipe.

Put one serving in a leak-proof leftover container as you clean up the kitchen after dinner, and you'll be ready to race out the door without any extra lunch preparation the next morning.

WEEK 1

SPICY SALMON (PAGE 19)

Breakfast: 2 slices whole grain toast topped with 2 tablespoons part-skim ricotta and ¼ cup fresh blueberries; or 1-2-3 breakfast of your choice (page 13)

Lunch: **Simple Bistro Salad** (recipe follows) with 1 whole grain pita and 1 orange

Dinner: **Spicy Salmon** (recipe follows) with asparagus roasted in olive oil and lemon juice, served with cooked farro (make extra for dinner on Day 3)

Dessert: 1 pear

SIMPLE BISTRO SALAD (SERVES 1)

It's easy to meet your daily vegetable goals with this hearty salad in your repertoire. We use eggs for protein, but feel free to swap in a scoop of tuna or beans.

- **2 cups mixed salad greens (like baby spinach, arugula, spring mix)**
- **½ cup cherry tomatoes, halved**
- **1 carrot, peeled and grated**
- **1 cucumber, sliced**
- **2 radishes, sliced**
- **2 hard-boiled eggs**
- **½ lemon, juiced**
- **½ tablespoon olive oil**
- **Salt and pepper, to taste**

Combine salad greens, tomatoes, carrot, cucumber, radishes, and eggs in a bowl. Cover with lemon juice, olive oil, salt and pepper; toss to combine.

SPICY SALMON (SERVES 4)

This spicy salmon recipe, first featured in our original Oldways 4-Week Mediterranean Diet Menu Plan book, is a staff favorite at Oldways.

- **4 cloves garlic, chopped**
- **½ teaspoon sea salt**
- **1 teaspoon crushed red pepper**
- **2 tablespoons extra-virgin olive oil**
- **1 lemon, juiced**
- **4 salmon steaks or fillets, each about 4 ounces**

Crush garlic and salt with a mortar and pestle or mash it with a fork in a small bowl. Add crushed red pepper, olive oil, and lemon juice; continue mashing to form a smooth paste. Arrange fish in a baking dish and spread this marinade on top.

Cover with plastic wrap and refrigerate for up to 2 hours.

Preheat oven to 450°F. Uncover fish and bake for about 20 minutes, or until the fish flakes easily with a fork.

Breakfast: 1 cup oatmeal with ½ cup milk, 1 teaspoon honey, and 1 tablespoon almonds, served with 1 medium banana and ½ cup plain Greek yogurt; or 1-2-3 breakfast of your choice (page 13)

Lunch: Leftover Spicy Salmon (page 19) mixed with hummus and spread on 2 slices whole grain bread with ½ cup baby carrots; or **Salmon Salad Sandwich** (recipe follows) served with ½ cup baby carrots

Dinner: **Whole Grain Spaghetti with Arugula Walnut Pesto** (recipe follows) served with a green salad with Vinaigrette (page 86)

Dessert: 1 cup grapes

SALMON SALAD SANDWICH (SERVES 1)

You can use leftover salmon from the Spicy Salmon (Day 1) instead of canned salmon. Or feel free to swap the canned salmon for canned tuna.

- **2 slices of whole grain bread**
- **3 ounces canned salmon**
- **1 celery stalk, finely chopped**
- **1 tablespoon plain Greek yogurt**
- **½ lemon**
- **Salt and pepper, to taste**
- **Handful of lettuce**

Combine salmon, celery, and yogurt in a bowl. Squeeze over lemon juice, sprinkle with salt and pepper. Mix well to combine.

Place salmon salad on one slice of bread. Top with handful of lettuce. Top with second slice of bread.

WHOLE GRAIN SPAGHETTI WITH ARUGULA WALNUT PESTO (SERVES 6)

This pesto does double duty, serving as both a nutty pasta sauce on Day 2 and an herbed sandwich spread on Day 3. Pesto also tastes great stirred into polenta or scrambled eggs.

- **12 ounces whole grain spaghetti**
- **3 cups baby arugula**
- **1 cup walnuts**
- **2 cloves of garlic, peeled**
- **¼ cup olive oil**
- **½ teaspoon salt**
- **2 cups canned navy beans, drained and rinsed**
- **Salt and pepper, to taste**

Cook pasta according to package instructions.

Using a food processor or blender, chop arugula and walnuts for 30 seconds. Add garlic, olive oil, and salt. Continue to blend until desired consistency.

If pesto is not smooth enough, add water a teaspoon at a time until consistency is saucy. Reserve ¼ cup pesto for lunch on Day 3.

Mix pasta and navy beans with remaining pesto.

Breakfast: ½ cup plain Greek yogurt topped with ½ cup pitted cherries and ¼ cup granola; or 1-2-3 breakfast of your choice (page 13)

Lunch: Leftover Whole Grain Pasta with Arugula Pesto (page 21); or **Pesto, Mozzarella, Tomato, and Arugula Sandwich** (recipe follows) served with sliced cucumbers

Dinner: **Lentil Soup** (recipe follows) with cooked farro (leftover from Day 1 dinner), served with a green salad with Yogurt-Herb Dressing (page 87)

Dessert: 1 pear served with 1 ounce Pecorino Romano (or other artisan cheese)

PESTO, MOZZARELLA, TOMATO, AND ARUGULA SANDWICH (SERVES 2)

Use the leftover pesto from Day 2 dinner.

- **4 tablespoons Arugula Walnut Pesto (leftover from Day 2 dinner)**
- **4 slices of whole grain bread, toasted**
- **2 ounces mozzarella cheese, sliced**
- **1 tomato, sliced**
- **1 cup arugula**

Spread 1 tablespoon of pesto on each slice of toast. Layer ½ cup arugula, ½ the tomato slices, and 1 ounce mozzarella cheese slices per sandwich. Top with the second slice of toast.

LENTIL SOUP (SERVES 4)

Don't let the simple-sounding ingredient list fool you; this classic dish packs a flavor punch.

- 2 tablespoons olive oil
- 1 large onion, chopped
- 1 stalk celery, chopped
- 1 garlic clove, minced
- 2 teaspoons ground cumin
- 2 tablespoons tomato paste
- 1 quart low-sodium vegetable or chicken stock
- 1 cup uncooked lentils
- 1 lemon, juiced
- Salt and pepper, to taste
- Crumbled feta cheese for garnish

Heat olive oil in a large pot over medium heat. Add onion, celery, and garlic; sauté for 2 minutes. Add the cumin and cook, stirring, for 1 minute longer. Add tomato paste and stir until smooth. Add the stock and lentils.

Bring just to a boil, reduce the heat, and simmer partially covered for 20 minutes, or until the lentils are very soft. Add 1 cup of water if the soup seems too thick.

Using a blender (in batches) or an immersion blender, blend the soup until smooth. Return soup to pot if necessary and stir in lemon juice. Season with salt and pepper. Serve garnished with feta cheese.

DAY 4

Breakfast: 1 whole grain English muffin with 2 slices of tomato and 1 tablespoon hummus, served with 1 cup melon cubes and 1 soft-boiled egg; or 1-2-3 breakfast of your choice (page 13)

Lunch: Leftover Lentil Soup (page 23) served with 1 apple and 1 ounce pistachios; or **Mediterranean Orzo Salad** (recipe follows)

Dinner: Artichoke and Spinach Frittata (recipe follows) served with sweet potato cut into wedges and roasted in olive oil

Dessert: Watermelon Granita (page 85)

MEDITERRANEAN ORZO SALAD (SERVES 6)

This lunchbox-friendly dish also travels well for picnics and potlucks.

- **1 small eggplant, diced**
- **1 bell pepper, diced**
- **1 red onion, diced**
- **2 tablespoons olive oil, divided**
- **1 tablespoon balsamic vinegar**
- **12 ounces whole grain orzo pasta (can substitute a different shape)**

- **1 lemon, juiced**
- **1 (15-ounce) can chickpeas, drained and rinsed**
- **4 ounces feta cheese, diced**
- **1 pint cherry tomatoes, halved**
- **¼ cup basil, sliced**

Preheat oven to 425°F. Toss eggplant, bell pepper, and onion with 1 tablespoon of oil and the vinegar, then roast for 40 minutes until browned, flipping halfway.

Cook orzo according to package instructions, then toss with remaining oil, lemon juice, roasted vegetables, chickpeas, feta, tomatoes, and basil.

ARTICHOKE AND SPINACH FRITTATA (SERVES 4)

Baked egg dishes, like the Italian frittata or Spanish tortilla, are common throughout the Mediterranean and can be eaten at breakfast, lunch, or dinner.

- **12 eggs**
- **½ cup low-fat milk**
- **2 cups baby spinach, chopped**
- **1 (15-ounce) can artichoke hearts, drained and chopped**
- **4 ounces Pecorino Romano cheese, grated (can substitute Parmigiano-Reggiano)**
- **Olive oil spray**

Preheat oven to 350°F. Coat a muffin tin with olive oil spray.

In a medium bowl, whisk together the eggs and milk. Evenly fill the bottom of the muffin tin with baby spinach and artichoke hearts. Pour the egg and milk mixture evenly into the muffin tin. Top each egg "muffin" with Pecorino Romano cheese.

Bake for 15-20 minutes, until cheese is melted and eggs are fully cooked. Serving size is 2 "muffins". If you don't have a muffin tin, you can use a 9x13" baking dish instead, though the baking time will be closer to 30-40 minutes.

Breakfast: ½ cup whole grain cereal with 1 tablespoon almonds and ½ cup milk, served with 1 cup berries; or 1-2-3 breakfast of your choice (page 13)

Lunch: Leftover Spinach and Artichoke Frittata (page 25); or **Meze Plate** (recipe follows)

Dinner: **Vegetable-Beef Kebabs** (recipe follows) served with brown rice

Dessert: 2 small clementines

MEZE PLATE (SERVES 1)

Meze (or Mezze) is an array of small dishes served as an appetizer or meal in many areas of the Mediterranean and Middle East.

- **2 tablespoons hummus**
- **2 tablespoons tabbouleh (page 52)**
- **2 tablespoons tzatziki**
- **2 tablespoons olives**
- **1 whole grain pita**

Arrange each of the ingredients on a large plate. Feel free to mix in raw vegetables or use the pita to scoop up the dips.

VEGETABLE-BEEF KEBABS (SERVES 4)

Pair meat with a number of other vegetables to keep these kebabs heart-healthy.

- **1 tablespoon olive oil**
- **1 teaspoon dried Italian herb seasoning**
- **2 cloves garlic, minced**
- **1 lemon, juiced**
- **½ pound sirloin**
- **1 red bell pepper**
- **1 green bell pepper**
- **1 onion**
- **6 large mushrooms, thickly sliced**
- **½ cup cherry tomatoes**

Combine the olive oil, seasoning, garlic, and lemon juice in a small baking dish and blend with a fork.

Cut the sirloin, peppers, and onion into chunks and add to the baking dish along with the sliced mushrooms. Toss and let sit at room temperature for 15 minutes.

Preheat the broiler or heat the grill. Thread the meat and vegetables onto skewers, leaving spaces in between the individual pieces so they will cook evenly. Cook for 4 minutes, turn, and cook for another 4-6 minutes. Serve hot or cold.

Breakfast: 1 egg scrambled with ½ ounce mozzarella cheese, 1 small tomato, and a handful of chopped fresh basil, served with 1 slice whole grain toast and 1 plum; or 1-2-3 breakfast of your choice (page 13)

Lunch: Leftover Vegetable-Beef Kebabs with brown rice (page 27); or **Meze Rollup** (recipe follows) served with 1 plum

Dinner: **Cauliflower with Chickpeas** (recipe follows) served with whole wheat couscous and a spinach salad with Balsamic Vinaigrette (page 86)

Dessert: 1 cup grapes

MEZE ROLLUP (SERVES 1)

Walnuts, hummus, and feta all contribute protein to this vegetarian wrap.

- **1 whole grain pita or tortilla**
- **2 tablespoons hummus**
- **1 large roasted red bell pepper, chopped**
- **2 tablespoons chopped walnuts**
- **¼ cup spinach**
- **1 tablespoon crumbled feta cheese**

Spread pita or tortilla with hummus, then fill it with roasted red pepper, chopped walnuts, spinach, and feta cheese. Roll into a wrap.

CAULIFLOWER WITH CHICKPEAS (SERVES 4)

Add a can of tuna to this quick dish, or substitute broccoli for the cauliflower.

- 2 tablespoons olive oil
- 1 onion, chopped
- 1 yellow squash, chopped
- 1 red bell pepper, seeded and chopped
- 1 small head cauliflower, broken into florets
- 1 teaspoon cumin
- 1 (14.5-ounce) can diced tomatoes
- 1 (15-ounce) can chickpeas, drained and rinsed

Heat olive oil in a large pot over medium heat. Add onion, squash, and pepper; sauté for about 5 minutes until the vegetables soften.

Add the cauliflower and cook for 5 minutes longer. Sprinkle in cumin and cook for 1 minute.

Add diced tomatoes and chickpeas; stir, and cook for 5 minutes longer or until the cauliflower is tender.

Breakfast: ½ cup plain Greek yogurt topped with ¼ cup granola and 1 sliced banana; or 1-2-3 breakfast of your choice (page 13)

Lunch: Leftover Cauliflower with Chickpeas with whole wheat couscous (page 29); or **Minestrone** (recipe follows) served with 1 slice whole grain bread and an arugula salad with walnuts and Lemon Vinaigrette (page 86)

Dinner: **Pasta with Broccoli and Chicken Sausage** (recipe follows) served with a green salad with Balsamic Vinaigrette (page 86)

Dessert: ½ cup fresh berries

MINESTRONE (SERVES 6)

Soup and salad is an easy lunchtime combination for those on a journey to healthier eating.

- 2 tablespoons olive oil
- 1 yellow onion, diced
- 2 carrots, peeled and chopped
- 2 stalks celery, chopped
- 2-3 cloves garlic, minced
- 1 pound spinach, chopped
- 1 large potato, peeled and chopped
- 1 (14.5-ounce) can diced tomatoes
- 2 teaspoons dried rosemary
- 4 cups low-sodium chicken stock
- ½ cup small dried pasta
- 1 (15-ounce) can cannellini beans, drained and rinsed
- Salt and pepper, to taste

Heat olive oil in a large pot over medium heat. Add onion, carrots, celery, and garlic; sauté for about 5 minutes until the vegetables soften.

Add spinach and potato and sauté for 2 minutes longer. Add tomatoes and rosemary and simmer for about 5 minutes, until the spinach is wilted. Add the stock and bring to a boil.

Add the pasta, reduce the heat to medium and cook until the potato and pasta are tender, about 10 minutes. Stir in the beans and simmer for 5 minutes. Season with salt and pepper.

PASTA WITH CHICKEN SAUSAGE AND ROASTED BROCCOLI (SERVES 4)

Pasta dishes are a great way to ease yourself into smaller portions of meat.

- **8 ounces whole grain pasta, like penne or fusili**
- **2 tablespoons olive oil, divided**
- **1 pound broccoli, chopped**
- **4 chicken sausages, sliced into ½ inch-thick rounds**
- **¼ cup sundried tomatoes, chopped**

Cook pasta according to package instructions. Preheat oven to 375°F and line a large baking sheet with aluminum foil.

Toss broccoli with 1 tablespoon olive oil and spread evenly on baking sheet. Roast broccoli for 20-30 minutes, until crisp.

Meanwhile, heat a large skillet over medium heat and add remaining 1 tablespoon olive oil. Add chicken sausage slices. Cook for 5 minutes, until browned. Add broccoli, sundried tomatoes, and pasta to the pan; mix well.

Breakfast: **Apricot Tahini Oatmeal:** 1 cup cooked oatmeal topped with 4 chopped dried apricots, 1 tablespoon tahini, and 1 teaspoon honey, served with ½ cup plain Greek yogurt; or 1-2-3 breakfast of your choice (page 13)

Lunch: Leftover Pasta with Chicken Sausage and Roasted Broccoli (page 31) served with a green salad with Balsamic Vinaigrette (page 86); or **Fennel, Orange, and Beet Salad** (recipe follows)

Dinner: **Six-Minute Shrimp with Whole Grain Linguine** (recipe follows) served with a mixed greens salad with Avocado Dressing (page 87)

Dessert: ½ cup plain Greek yogurt with 2 teaspoons honey and sprinkle of walnuts

FENNEL, ORANGE, AND BEET SALAD (SERVES 4)

This vibrant colors (and flavors!) in this salad are sure to delight guests.

- **8 cups of spring salad mix**
- **1 fennel bulb, thinly sliced**
- **2 oranges, thinly sliced**
- **1 avocado, cut into chunks**
- **2 cups canned sliced beets, no salt added, rinsed, drained, and cut into half moons**
- **1 cup thinly sliced cucumber**
- **½ cup chopped roasted pecan halves**
- **1 cup cooked chickpeas, drained and rinsed**
- **½ cup crumbled feta cheese**
- **2 tablespoons olive oil**
- **2 tablespoons balsamic vinegar**

Combine all ingredients in a large bowl and toss well.

SIX-MINUTE SHRIMP WITH
WHOLE GRAIN LINGUINE (SERVES 4)

Here's a very easy way to cook shrimp, whether fresh or frozen.

- **8 ounces whole grain linguine**
- **2 tablespoons extra-virgin olive oil**
- **2 cloves garlic, chopped**
- **1 onion, sliced**
- **1 pound fresh shrimp (about 25), peeled, or 1 pound frozen shrimp, thawed for 5 minutes in cold water**
- **1 teaspoon dried thyme**
- **Salt and pepper, to taste**

Cook pasta according to package instructions. Arrange the oven rack so it is about 8 inches from the heat source and heat the broiler.

Heat olive oil in a large cast iron or ovenproof skillet over medium heat. Add garlic and onion; cook about 3 minutes. Add shrimp and thyme, season with salt and pepper, and toss gently to mix evenly.

Place the skillet under the broiler and cook for about 3 minutes. Stir, then cook for another 3 minutes, or until the shrimp turn pink. Add pasta to the skillet and mix well.

Breakfast: 1 egg scrambled with 1 ounce feta and ½ cup sliced spinach, placed in a whole grain pita with 1 small sliced tomato, served with 1 orange; or 1-2-3 breakfast of your choice (page 13)

Lunch: Leftover Six-Minute Shrimp with Whole Grain Linguine (page 35); or **Hearty Tomato Soup with Citrus Cod** (recipe follows) served with 1 whole grain roll or 1 slice whole grain bread

Dinner: **Chicken Kebabs with Yogurt Sauce** (recipe follows) served with whole wheat couscous (make extra for lunch on Day 10) and roasted broccoli with lemon juice and olive oil

Dessert: 1 apple

HEARTY TOMATO SOUP WITH CITRUS COD (SERVES 4)

This robust soup is filled with veggies. Use a whole grain roll to soak up every last bit of it!

- **1 tablespoon olive oil**
- **1 onion, chopped**
- **1 fennel bulb, chopped**
- **2 (28-ounce) cans of whole plum tomatoes**
- **1 pint low-sodium vegetable broth**
- **1 pound cod, cut into 4-ounce fillets**
- **1 orange, sliced**
- **Salt and pepper, to taste**

Preheat oven to 400°F. Heat olive oil in a medium pot over medium heat. Add onions and cook until translucent, approximately 5-7 minutes. Add fennel and cook for 5-7 minutes, until lightly browned. Add both cans of tomatoes, including the juice. Using a wooden spoon, break tomatoes into chunks. Heat for 2 minutes. Add the broth and bring to a boil. Simmer for 5 minutes.

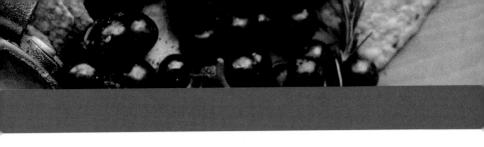

While soup simmers, place cod fillets on an aluminum foil-lined baking sheet. Top each slice of cod with a few slices of orange, salt, and pepper. Cook cod for 15-20 minutes, until opaque. Discard orange slices.

Using a blender (in batches) or an immersion blender, blend the soup until smooth. Season soup with salt and pepper. Evenly distribute soup into four bowls and top each bowl with a fillet of cod.

CHICKEN KEBABS WITH YOGURT SAUCE (SERVES 4)

Here's an easy way to cook chicken. You can also serve the skewers on top of lettuce, along with some whole grain pita bread and sliced tomatoes.

- **1 cup plain Greek yogurt**
- **3 cloves garlic, minced**
- **1 tablespoon chopped fresh dill or 1 teaspoon dried dill**
- **1 lemon, juiced**
- **1 teaspoon cumin**
- **1 pound boneless, skinless chicken breasts**

Combine the yogurt, garlic, dill, lemon juice, and cumin in a bowl and stir until smooth. Set aside about half of the sauce. Cut the chicken into 1-inch chunks and add to the bowl with the remaining sauce. Toss and set aside for 10 minutes.

Preheat the broiler or heat the grill. Thread the chicken onto skewers and cook for 5 minutes. Turn and cook for another 4 minutes, until internal temperature of chicken reaches 165°F. Serve with the set-aside sauce for dipping, saving 2 tablespoons for Chickpea Salad (Day 10).

Breakfast: 1 slice whole grain cinnamon-raisin bread spread with 1 tablespoon peanut butter or almond butter, served with 4 small fresh figs and 1 hard-boiled egg; or 1-2-3 breakfast of your choice (page 13)

Lunch: Leftover Chicken Kebabs (page 37), whole wheat couscous, and roasted broccoli; or **Chickpea Salad** (recipe follows) over whole wheat couscous (use leftover couscous from dinner on Day 9), served with ½ cup plain Greek yogurt topped with 2 teaspoons honey and 1 tablespoon almonds

Dinner: **Mussels Provençal** (recipe follows) with whole grain linguine, served with green beans and an arugula salad with goat cheese and Balsamic Vinaigrette (page 86)

Dessert: 1 cup cubed cantaloupe

CHICKPEA SALAD (SERVES 2)

We're serving this chickpea salad atop whole wheat couscous, although it also tastes great stuffed in a whole grain pita.

- **1 medium cucumber, diced**
- **1 cup cooked chickpeas**
- **1 cup cherry tomatoes, halved**
- **2 tablespoons Yogurt Sauce (leftover from Day 9 dinner)**

Combine all ingredients in a bowl and toss well.

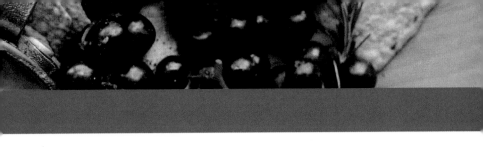

MUSSELS PROVENÇAL (SERVES 4)

Mussels are easy to cook, and they're one of the most sustainable seafood choices.

- **8 ounces whole grain linguine**
- **3 pounds mussels**
- **1 cup dry white wine**
- **2 cloves garlic, finely minced**
- **1 small onion, diced**
- **1 stalk celery, diced**
- **1 large tomato, diced**
- **Salt and pepper, to taste**

Cook pasta according to package instructions. Soak mussels in cold water and scrub to remove any dirt. Remove any hairy "beards" with a sharp knife. Drain.

Combine wine, garlic, onions, celery, and tomato in a large pot and bring just to a boil over high heat. Add mussels; cover, reduce heat to medium, and cook for about 10 minutes until the mussels have opened.

Using tongs, transfer mussels to four large bowls (discard any that have not opened) along with linguine. Pour the broth remaining in the pot into a saucepan and boil for about 3 minutes. Season with salt and pepper, and pour the broth over the mussels.

Breakfast: 1 cup whole grain cereal with 1 cup strawberries and ½ cup plain Greek yogurt; or 1-2-3 breakfast of your choice (page 13)

Lunch: Leftover Mussels Provençal with whole grain linguine and green beans (page 39); or **Fattoush** (recipe follows)

Dinner: **Polenta with Greens and Fried Eggs** (recipe follows)

Dessert: 4 dried apricots served with 1 ounce almonds

FATTOUSH (SERVES 2)

This simple yet tasty salad uses torn pita bread as a main ingredient. It's a great way to use up bread that's just starting to get stale.

- 2 cups Romaine lettuce
- 3 radishes, chopped
- 2 scallions, chopped
- 1 medium tomato, chopped
- 1 small cucumber, chopped
- ¼ cup parsley, chopped
- 1 small green pepper, chopped
- 1 whole grain pita
- 2 teaspoons lemon juice
- 1 tablespoon olive oil
- ¼ cup crumbled feta cheese

Combine lettuce, radishes, scallions, tomato, cucumber, parsley, and green pepper in a bowl and toss gently.

Tear pita into small bits, add to the salad, and toss again. Sprinkle the salad with lemon juice and olive oil; toss, and garnish with feta cheese.

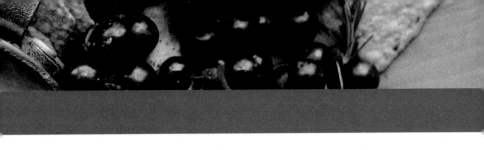

POLENTA WITH GREENS AND FRIED EGGS (SERVES 4)

This dish is best served fresh, so cut the recipe in half if you're only cooking for two.

- **1 cup whole grain polenta**
- **½ cup Pecorino Romano cheese, grated**
- **2 bunches Swiss chard, chopped**
- **2 garlic cloves, sliced**
- **1 tablespoon olive oil, divided**
- **8 eggs**
- **Salt and pepper, to taste**

Cook polenta according to package instructions. Slowly stir in Pecorino Romano cheese until melted and thoroughly incorporated.

Heat ½ tablespoon olive oil in a medium skillet over medium-low heat. Add garlic and cook for 30 seconds. Add Swiss chard and cook for 2-4 minutes, until wilted. Season with salt and pepper.

Heat remaining ½ tablespoon olive oil in a non-stick skillet over medium heat. Cook 2 eggs over-medium (until egg whites are opaque, but yolk is still runny). Repeat with remaining eggs.

To serve, evenly distribute polenta into four bowls, topped with Swiss chard. Place 2 eggs on top of each polenta-greens tower.

DAY 12

WEEK 1 2 3 4

Breakfast: 1 cup cooked oatmeal topped with cinnamon, 1 diced peach, 2 tablespoons part-skim ricotta, and 1 tablespoon chopped walnuts; or 1-2-3 breakfast of your choice (page 13)

Lunch: **Roasted Butternut Squash Soup** (recipe follows) served with 1 whole grain roll, ½ cup plain Greek yogurt with 1 teaspoon honey, and 2 tablespoons fresh berries

Dinner: **Chicken with Romesco Sauce** (recipe follows) served with brown rice and green beans

Dessert: 1 pear

ROASTED BUTTERNUT SQUASH SOUP (SERVES 4)

This soup is the perfect balance of sweet and savory. We suggest reserving half of the roasted butternut squash to repurpose into dinner on Day 13.

- **2 small butternut squash, peeled and cubed**

- **1 onion, chopped**

- **2 apples, peeled and chopped**

- **2 tablespoons olive oil, divided**

- **1 pint low-sodium chicken broth**

- **1 cup water**

- **Salt and pepper, to taste**

Preheat oven to 375°F and line a large baking sheet with aluminum foil. Toss butternut squash with 1 tablespoon olive oil and spread evenly on baking sheet. Roast butternut squash for 30 minutes until tender and lightly browned. Reserve half of butternut squash for Roasted Butternut Squash Pasta (Day 13).

42

While squash roasts, heat 1 tablespoon olive oil in a large pot over medium heat. Add onion and sauté until translucent. Add chopped apples and sauté another 5 minutes. Add roasted squash to the pot, along with the broth and water. Bring to a boil and simmer for 5-10 minutes.

Using a blender (in batches) or an immersion blender, blend the soup until smooth. Add water as necessary for desired consistency. Season with salt and pepper.

CHICKEN WITH ROMESCO SAUCE (SERVES 4)

This versatile, Spanish-inspired sauce is also great as a dipping sauce for grilled vegetables, or tossed with whole grain pasta.

- **¼ cup tomato paste**
- **2 large roasted red bell peppers**
- **2 garlic cloves, peeled**
- **¼ cup almonds**
- **¼ cup fresh parsley**
- **2 tablespoons apple cider vinegar**

- **¼ cup olive oil**
- **2 teaspoons paprika**
- **¼ teaspoon cayenne**
- **½ teaspoon cumin**
- **1½ pounds boneless, skinless chicken breast, cooked, and diced or shredded into bite-sized pieces**

Add all ingredients except chicken to a food processor or blender and pulse until well-combined (yields about 1 ⅓ cups sauce). Reserve 2 tablespoons for Spanish Picnic (Day 14).

Heat a large skillet over medium-low heat. Add 1 cup of the Romesco sauce and chicken and stir until chicken is coated, and dish is warmed through.

Breakfast: 1 egg scrambled in 1 tablespoon olive oil with 1 small tomato and ½ ounce crumbled feta cheese, served with 1 cup blackberries and 1 slice whole grain toast; or 1-2-3 breakfast of your choice (page 13)

Lunch: Leftover Chicken with Romesco Sauce served with brown rice and green beans (page 43); or **Roasted Red Pepper and Avocado Tartine** (recipe follows) served with 1 ounce almonds

Dinner: **Roasted Butternut Squash Pasta** (recipe follows) served with a green salad with Herb Vinaigrette (page 86)

Dessert: Grilled (or baked) peaches

ROASTED RED PEPPER AND AVOCADO TARTINE (SERVES 2)

A tartine, an elaborate open-faced sandwich, is a common morning or mid-day meal in France.

- **½ cup plain Greek yogurt**
- **1 roasted red bell pepper, diced**
- **¼ teaspoon freshly cracked black pepper**
- **4 slices of whole grain bread, toasted**
- **1 avocado, sliced**
- **½ teaspoon za'atar seasoning**

In a small bowl, mix together the yogurt, roasted red pepper, and black pepper. Spread each slice of toast with about 2 tablespoons of the yogurt mixture, then top with avocado slices.

Finish each tartine with a pinch of za'atar seasoning.

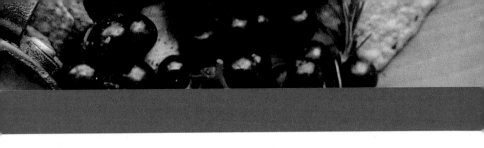

ROASTED BUTTERNUT SQUASH PASTA (SERVES 4)

This dish tastes especially good with crumbled Gorgonzola cheese, but feel free to use a different cheese - like goat, feta, or mozzarella - if you prefer!

- 8 ounces whole grain pasta, like penne or fusili
- ½ of butternut squash from Roasted Butternut Squash Soup recipe (Day 12 lunch)
- 1 tablespoon olive oil
- 2 garlic cloves, minced
- ½ teaspoon red pepper flakes
- ¼ cup parsley, chopped
- ¼ cup chopped walnuts
- 4 ounces Gorgonzola cheese, crumbled
- Salt and pepper, to taste

Cook pasta according to package. Heat olive oil in a medium skillet over medium heat. Add garlic and red pepper flakes; cook for 30 seconds. Add roasted butternut squash and cook for 5 minutes, long enough to reheat the squash.

Once pasta is finished cooking, add pasta and 2 tablespoons of pasta water to skillet. Add chopped parsley, walnuts, and Gorgonzola; stir to combine. Season with salt and pepper.

DAY 14

Breakfast: Veggie Omelet (page 76) served with 1 orange and 1 slice whole grain toast; or 1-2-3 breakfast of your choice (page 13)

Lunch: Leftover Roasted Butternut Squash Pasta (page 45) served with a green salad with Honey-Mustard Vinaigrette (page 86); or **Spanish Picnic** (recipe follows) served with 1 whole grain roll

Dinner: Lemon and Caper Cod with Potatoes (recipe follows) served with a mixed greens salad with Vinaigrette (page 86)

Dessert: ¼ cup dried cherries served with 1 ounce Manchego cheese (or other traditional artisan cheese)

SPANISH PICNIC (SERVES 1)

If you can't find Marcona almonds, regular almonds (or other nuts, like pistachios or walnuts) are also a good choice.

- **¼ cup radishes**
- **¼ cup carrot sticks**
- **2 tablespoons Romesco Sauce (leftover from Day 12 dinner)**
- **½ ounce Manchego cheese or sharp cheddar**
- **¼ cup Marcona almonds**

Arrange each of the ingredients on a large plate. The Romesco is a great dip for the carrots and radishes.

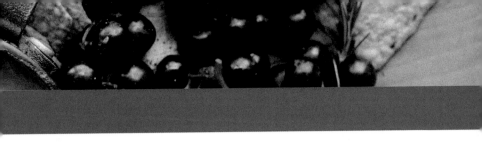

LEMON AND CAPER COD WITH POTATOES (SERVES 4)

The lemony dill dressing is the perfect complement to this seafood dish.

- **1 pound cod, cut into four 4-ounce fillets**
- **2 lemons, divided (1 sliced, 1 juiced)**
- **¼ cup capers, divided**
- **1 pound new potatoes, cubed**
- **1 red onion, cubed**
- **3 tablespoons olive oil, divided**
- **¼ cup fresh dill, chopped**
- **Salt and pepper, to taste**

Preheat oven to 400°F and line two baking sheets with aluminum foil.

Toss potatoes, red onion, and 1 tablespoon of olive oil in a bowl. Spread evenly over baking sheet and bake for 20-30 minutes, until potatoes are fork-tender.

Meanwhile, place cod fillets on other baking sheet. Evenly spread lemon slices from 1 lemon over fillets. Drizzle 1 tablespoon olive oil and sprinkle 2 tablespoons capers over the fillets.

Bake the cod for 12-15 minutes, until fork-tender and opaque.

In a medium bowl, whisk remaining 1 tablespoon olive oil, lemon juice, dill, and 2 tablespoons of capers together.

Pour the cooked potatoes and onions into the bowl and coat evenly with dressing. Season with salt and pepper. Distribute potato and onion mixture evenly onto four plates; top with a cod fillet.

TABBOULEH (PAGE 52)

Breakfast: 2 slices of whole grain toast topped with ½ mashed avocado, ¼ cup arugula, and 1 sliced hard-boiled egg, served with ½ cup fresh berries; or 1-2-3 breakfast of your choice (page 13)

Lunch: Leftover Lemon and Caper Cod with Potatoes (page 47) served with a mixed greens salad with Honey-Mustard Vinaigrette (page 86); or **Massaged Kale Salad with Farro and Sweet Potato** (recipe follows)

Dinner: **Spinach-Mushroom Strata** (recipe follows) served with a mixed greens salad with Avocado Dressing (page 87)

Dessert: 1 cup fresh honeydew melon

MASSAGED KALE SALAD WITH FARRO AND SWEET POTATO (SERVES 4)

This recipe can be easily varied. Try a different grain (like quinoa, wheat berries, or bulgur), fruit (like figs, grapes, or pears), nuts/seeds, and cheese. The combinations are endless!

- ½ cup farro
- 1 sweet potato, chopped
- 1 pound kale, stems removed and leaves chopped
- 3 tablespoons olive oil, divided
- 1 lemon, juiced
- ½ teaspoon salt
- 1 apple, chopped
- ¼ cup sunflower seeds
- ¼ cup almonds
- 1 (15-ounce) can chickpeas, drained and rinsed
- ¼ cup crumbled feta cheese

Cook farro according to package instructions. Preheat oven to 375°F and line a large baking sheet with aluminum foil.

Toss sweet potato with 1 tablespoon olive oil and spread evenly on baking sheet. Roast sweet potato for 20-30 minutes, until fork-tender.

Meanwhile, add chopped kale to a large bowl. Add 2 remaining tablespoons of olive oil, lemon juice, and salt to the bowl. Using both hands, massage the kale for 2 minutes. The kale should turn a dark green color and will feel smooth, rather than coarse.

Add apples, sunflower seeds, almonds, chickpeas, and feta to the bowl. Mix well. Once farro and sweet potato have cooled, add them to the bowl and mix well.

SPINACH-MUSHROOM STRATA (SERVES 6)

Plan ahead to make this delicious and economical dish, which is a great way to use up bread before it turns stale. If you can't find Fontina Val d'Aosta cheese, try Gruyère, Gouda, or Provolone.

- **1 (10-ounce) package frozen spinach, thawed**
- **1 tablespoon olive oil**
- **1 cup sliced mushrooms**
- **4 eggs**
- **2 cups 1% milk**
- **1 teaspoon Dijon mustard**
- **6 slices thick, day-old whole grain bread, cut into cubes**
- **1¼ cups grated Fontina Val d'Aosta cheese**

Lightly grease a two-quart baking dish and set aside. Squeeze spinach to remove moisture, then chop finely. Heat olive oil in a skillet and sauté mushrooms for about 4 minutes, until soft. Add spinach and cook for 2 minutes longer. Beat eggs with milk and mustard.

To assemble, layer half the bread cubes into the bottom of the baking dish. Top with mushrooms and spinach, and sprinkle with 1 cup of cheese. Cover with remaining bread cubes. Pour egg mixture over the top and press down gently with a spatula. Sprinkle on remaining ¼ cup of cheese. Cover with plastic wrap and refrigerate overnight. Preheat oven to 350°F. Uncover the strata and bake for 30-45 minutes, until browned.

DAY 16

Breakfast: 2 whole grain English muffin halves each topped with ½ a small sliced tomato, ½ a hard-boiled egg, ½ tablespoon crumbled feta, and a pinch of dried oregano, served with 1 pear; or 1-2-3 breakfast of your choice (page 13)

Lunch: Leftover Spinach-Mushroom Strata (page 51) served with a mixed greens salad with Avocado Dressing (page 87); or **Tabbouleh** (recipe follows) served with ¼ cup hummus, 1 sliced bell pepper, and 1 whole grain pita

Dinner: **Herb-Baked Fish** (recipe follows) served with bulgur and olive oil-roasted carrots

Dessert: ½ cup fresh berries

TABBOULEH (SERVES 2)

Here's a great way to use up fresh parsley. Garnish with feta if you wish, and add diced cucumber, diced celery, or chopped scallions. Bulgur comes in various "grinds" ranging from fine to coarse. The coarser the grind, the more texture your salad will have.

- **½ cup cooked bulgur**
- **1 tablespoon lemon juice**
- **1 garlic clove, minced**
- **1 cup fresh parsley, chopped**
- **¼ cup fresh mint, chopped (optional)**
- **1 medium tomato, diced**
- **Salt and pepper, to taste**

Combine warm cooked bulgur, lemon juice, and garlic and chill for 30 minutes. Add remaining ingredients, season with salt and pepper, and toss gently.

HERB-BAKED FISH (SERVES 4)

Get into the habit of serving fish to your family at least twice a week. It's a good source of protein and exposes kids to the world beyond burgers.

- **1 pound fresh halibut, cod, or salmon**
- **2 teaspoons olive oil**
- **1 teaspoon dried thyme**
- **¼ cup grated Parmigiano-Reggiano cheese**

Preheat oven to 425°F. Place fish in a flat baking dish, skin side down. Rub both sides with olive oil. Sprinkle top with thyme and cheese.

Bake for 10 minutes, or until fish flakes easily with a fork. Serve immediately.

Breakfast: ½ cup plain Greek yogurt topped with ½ cup strawberries and ¼ cup granola; or 1-2-3 breakfast of your choice (page 13)

Lunch: Leftover Herb-Baked Fish served with bulgur and roasted carrots (page 53); or **Hummus and Garden Veggie Sandwich** (recipe follows) served with 1 cup cubed cantaloupe

Dinner: **Pasta with Fresh Tomatoes and Basil** (recipe follows) served with sautéed greens (like kale, spinach, or chard)

Dessert: 1 orange

HUMMUS AND GARDEN VEGGIE SANDWICH (SERVES 1)

Add some turkey, prosciutto, or canned tuna for a heartier sandwich.

- **2 slices of whole grain bread**
- **2 tablespoons hummus**
- **¼ avocado, mashed**
- **1 ounce Kasseri or Provolone cheese, sliced**
- **½ cup baby spinach**
- **¼ cup sliced raw veggies (like carrots or cucumber)**

Spread hummus on one slice of bread and avocado on the other slice. Place cheese on top of the hummus, followed by baby spinach and veggies. Top with the bread that has the avocado spread on it.

PASTA WITH FRESH TOMATOES AND BASIL (SERVES 4)

Basil is easy to grow in a container near a window. With a small herb garden at your fingertips, it is easy to transform pantry staples like pasta and beans into fresh, fragrant meals.

- 8 ounces whole grain pasta, like penne or fusili
- 1 pint cherry tomatoes, halved
- 2 tablespoons extra-virgin olive oil
- ½ cup basil, chopped
- 1 garlic clove, minced
- 1 cup canned navy beans, drained and rinsed
- 4 ounces Pecorino Romano cheese, grated
- Salt and pepper, to taste

Cook pasta according to package instructions. Meanwhile, combine tomatoes, olive oil, basil, garlic, and navy beans in a large bowl.

Add cooked pasta to large bowl and mix well to combine. Season with salt and pepper. Serve topped with grated cheese.

Breakfast: 1 slice whole grain toast spread with 1 tablespoon goat cheese, served with 1 pear and 1 hard-boiled egg; or 1-2-3 breakfast of your choice (page 13)

Lunch: Leftover Pasta with Fresh Tomatoes and Basil served with sautéed greens (page 55); or **Fig and Manchego Sandwich** (recipe follows) served with sliced bell peppers and ¼ cup hummus

Dinner: Whole Grain Panzanella Salad with Tomatoes and Olives (recipe follows)

Dessert: ½ cup fresh berries

FIG AND MANCHEGO SANDWICH (SERVES 1)

Add some prosciutto or roasted turkey for a bit more protein.

- **2 slices of whole grain bread, toasted**
- **2 tablespoons fig jam**
- **1 ounce Manchego cheese, thinly sliced**
- **Handful of arugula**

Spread 1 tablespoon fig jam on each slice of toast. Place Manchego cheese slices on one slice of toast and top with arugula. Top with the other slice of toast and enjoy!

WHOLE GRAIN PANZANELLA SALAD WITH TOMATOES AND OLIVES (SERVES 4)

Feel free to add additional veggies to the salad, like roasted eggplant, zucchini, summer squash, or even corn.

- 1 small rustic whole grain loaf of bread (about ½ pound), chopped into cubes
- 2 chicken sausages, cut into ½-inch slices
- 4 medium tomatoes, coarsely chopped
- ⅓ cup olive oil
- 3 tablespoons red wine vinegar
- 2 garlic cloves, minced
- 1 red bell pepper, diced
- ¼ cup pitted Kalamata olives, halved
- 1 large bunch of basil, chopped

Preheat oven to 350°F. Place chopped bread onto a baking sheet and bake for 5-10 minutes, until lightly browned. Remove from oven and cool.

Meanwhile, heat a skillet over medium heat. Add sausage and cook until browned all over. Remove from heat and cool.

Combine tomatoes, olive oil, vinegar, garlic, bell pepper, olives, and basil in a bowl. Add bread and chicken sausage. Mix well to combine.

Breakfast: ½ cup plain Greek yogurt topped with 2 tablespoons each fruit preserves (such as fig jam), raisins, and chopped, toasted hazelnuts, served with 1 slice whole grain English muffin; or 1-2-3 breakfast of your choice (page 13)

Lunch: Leftover Whole Grain Panzanella Salad with Tomatoes and Olives (page 57); or **Roasted Cauliflower Soup** (recipe follows) served with ¼ cup hummus, ½ cup whole grain crackers, and 1 pear

Dinner: **Rosemary Roasted Chicken** (recipe follows) served with freekeh or bulgur and olive oil-sautéed broccoli rabe with lemon

Dessert: 2 small clementines

ROASTED CAULIFLOWER SOUP (SERVES 4)

When roasting cauliflower for this soup on Day 19, we roast extra to repurpose into pasta on Day 20.

- **2 large cauliflowers, chopped**
- **2 tablespoons olive oil, separated**
- **1 onion, chopped**
- **1 pint low-sodium chicken broth**
- **1 cup water**
- **Salt and pepper, to taste**

Preheat oven to 375°F and line a large baking sheet with aluminum foil. Toss cauliflower with 1 tablespoon olive oil and spread evenly on baking sheet. Roast cauliflower for 20-30 minutes, until crisp.

While cauliflower roasts, heat 1 tablespoon olive oil in a large pot over medium heat. Add onion and sauté until translucent. Add ½ of roasted cauliflower to the pot, along with the broth and 1 cup of water.

Reserve the other half of cauliflower for Roasted Cauliflower Pasta (Day 20).

Bring soup to a boil and simmer for 5-10 minutes. Using a blender (in batches) or an immersion blender, blend the soup until smooth. Add water as necessary for desired consistency. Season with salt and pepper.

ROSEMARY ROASTED CHICKEN (SERVES 4)

If you're new to roasting whole chickens, there are plenty of instructional videos on YouTube. You can repurpose any leftover chicken into the Chicken Caesar Salad on Day 21.

- **1 whole chicken (4 pounds)**
- **2 tablespoons olive oil**
- **Salt and pepper, to taste**
- **2 tablespoons chopped fresh rosemary**
- **1 lemon, halved**

Drizzle chicken with olive oil, then season inside and out with pepper and a generous amount of salt and rosemary. Squeeze juice of ½ lemon over the chicken, then stuff the interior of the chicken with remains of the lemon halves. (If you have time, refrigerate chicken uncovered for an hour, or overnight.)

Place chicken breast side up in a roasting pan and tie the legs together with kitchen twine, if available. Roast for 50-60 minutes, or until a thermometer reads 165°F when inserted in the thickest part of the thigh.

Breakfast: 2 whole grain English muffin halves with 1 tablespoon peanut butter, 1 banana, and ½ cup plain Greek yogurt; or 1-2-3 breakfast of your choice (page 13)

Lunch: Leftover Cauliflower Soup (page 58) served with an arugula salad with Herb Vinaigrette (page 86); or **Smoked Salmon Sandwich** (recipe follows) served with cucumber slices

Dinner: **Roasted Cauliflower Pasta** (recipe follows) served with an arugula salad with Herb Vinaigrette (page 86)

Dessert: 1 cup honeydew melon

SMOKED SALMON SANDWICH (SERVES 1)

The avocado in this sandwich is a healthier, tastier replacement for cream cheese. A few capers are a great addition. This recipe is also great for breakfast or brunch.

- **2 slices of whole grain bread**
- **2 ounces smoked salmon**
- **½ avocado, mashed**
- **½ cup arugula**
- **½ lemon**

Spread avocado on both slices of bread. Layer smoked salmon and arugula on top of one slice. Squeeze over lemon juice and top with the other bread slice.

ROASTED CAULIFLOWER PASTA (SERVES 4)

Try this recipe with pine nuts or hazelnuts as well as walnuts.

- 8 ounces whole grain pasta, like penne or fusili
- ½ of cauliflower from Roasted Cauliflower Soup recipe (Day 19 lunch)
- 1 tablespoon olive oil
- 2 garlic cloves, minced
- ½ teaspoon red pepper flakes
- ¼ cup parsley, chopped
- ¼ cup chopped walnuts
- 4 ounces Pecorino Romano cheese, grated
- Salt and pepper to taste

Cook pasta according to package instructions and reserve 2 tablespoons of pasta water.

Heat olive oil in a medium skillet over medium heat. Add garlic and red pepper flakes; cook for 30 seconds. Add roasted cauliflower and cook for 5 minutes, long enough to reheat the cauliflower.

Add pasta and reserved pasta water to skillet. Add chopped parsley and walnuts; stir to combine. Season with salt and pepper. Serve topped with grated cheese.

DAY 21

Breakfast: 1 whole grain pita filled with 1 scrambled egg, ½ cup halved cherry tomatoes, and 1 tablespoon goat cheese, served with 1 cup watermelon cubes; or 1-2-3 breakfast of your choice (page 13)

Lunch: Leftover Roasted Cauliflower Pasta (page 61) served with an arugula salad with Herb Vinaigrette (page 86); or **Chicken Caesar Salad** (recipe below) served with 1 whole grain pita

Dinner: **Sardine Puttanesca** (recipe follows) served with a spinach salad with Balsamic Vinaigrette (page 86)

Dessert: 1 biscotti cookie (store-bought or your favorite recipe)

CHICKEN CAESAR SALAD (SERVES 1)

Feel free to incorporate other vegetables you may have on hand, such as sliced celery, radishes, cucumbers, or cherry tomatoes. A fresh shaving of Pecorino Romano (leftover from Day 20) also adds a delicious touch.

- **½ head romaine lettuce, chopped**
- **⅓ cup cooked chicken, shredded or diced (leftover from Day 19 dinner)**
- **2 tablespoons Caesar Dressing (page 87)**

Combine lettuce and chicken in a large bowl. Drizzle dressing over the salad and toss until well-combined.

SARDINE PUTTANESCA (SERVES 4)

This dish is perfect for when you don't know what to make for dinner. Almost all of the ingredients can be found in your pantry, so it's a great end-of-the-week dish for when you haven't had time to go to the grocery store.

- **8 ounces whole grain penne pasta**
- **1 onion, chopped**
- **1 tablespoon olive oil**
- **1 teaspoon tomato paste**
- **2 (3-ounce) cans of sardines in olive oil, drained**
- **1 tablespoon capers**
- **1 tablespoon parsley, chopped**
- **Salt and pepper, to taste**

Cook pasta according to package instructions and reserve ½ cup pasta water to add to the sauce.

Heat olive oil in a medium-sized skillet over medium heat. Add onion and cook for 5-8 minutes, until translucent.

Add tomato paste and mix until onions are evenly coated. Add sardines; separate and mash with a wooden spoon. Add capers and pasta to skillet. Add reserved pasta water and mix to coat pasta. Top with parsley and season with salt and pepper.

Breakfast: 1 cup cooked oatmeal with ¼ cup walnuts, 2 tablespoons raisins, and 1 diced apple, served with ½ cup plain Greek yogurt; or 1-2-3 breakfast of your choice (page 13)

Lunch: Leftover Sardine Puttanesca (page 63); or **Tomato Basil Quinoa** (recipe follows); serve both options with a mixed greens salad with Avocado Dressing (page 87)

Dinner: Eggplant, Feta, Bulgur, and Chickpea Salad (recipe follows)

Dessert: ½ cup plain Greek yogurt topped with ¼ cup halved grapes and 1 teaspoon honey

TOMATO BASIL QUINOA (SERVES 4)

This is a terrific "quick and easy" meal to make. Add some grilled shrimp or chicken, if you need a bit more protein.

- **1 cup quinoa**
- **1 tablespoon olive oil**
- **2 garlic cloves, minced**
- **½ teaspoon red pepper flakes**
- **1 tablespoon tomato paste**
- **3 small tomatoes, diced**
- **1 bunch Swiss chard, chopped**
- **¼ cup basil, chopped**
- **1 cup canned navy beans, drained and rinsed**
- **4 ounces Pecorino Romano cheese, grated**
- **Salt and pepper, to taste**

Cook quinoa according to package instructions. Heat olive oil in a skillet over medium heat. Add garlic and red pepper flakes; stir for 1 minute. Add tomato paste and stir for another 1 minute. Add diced tomatoes and cook for 5 minutes. Add chopped Swiss chard and cook until wilted (3-5 minutes).

Stir in basil, beans, and cooked quinoa. Mix well, making sure everything is heated through (particularly the beans). Serve topped with grated cheese.

EGGPLANT, FETA, BULGUR, AND CHICKPEA SALAD (SERVES 4)

This salad tastes great the next day once the flavors have marinated overnight. Try other veggies like summer squash or portabella mushrooms.

- 1 eggplant, cubed
- 2 zucchini, diced
- 3 tablespoons olive oil, divided
- 1 cup bulgur
- 1 (15-ounce) can chickpeas, drained and rinsed

- ½ cup fresh mint, chopped
- 1 cup parsley, chopped
- ½ cup crumbled feta cheese
- 1 lemon, juiced
- ¼ cup pine nuts
- Salt and pepper, to taste

Preheat oven to 375°F. Line two baking sheets with aluminum foil.

Toss eggplant with 1 tablespoon olive oil in a medium bowl and spread evenly over one baking sheet. In the same bowl, toss zucchini with 1 tablespoon olive oil and spread evenly over second baking sheet. Bake vegetables for 20-30 minutes, until lightly browned and a fork-tender.

Cook bulgur according to package instructions. Combine cooked vegetables, bulgur, chickpeas, mint, parsley, and feta in a bowl. Drizzle remaining 1 tablespoon olive oil and lemon juice over bowl. Mix well to combine, season with salt and pepper. Top each serving with 1 tablespoon of pine nuts.

DAY 23

WEEK 1 2 3 **4**

Breakfast: 1 whole grain bagel with 1 ounce soft cheese (like Brie), served with ½ cup fresh raspberries; or 1-2-3 breakfast of your choice (page 13)

Lunch: Leftover Eggplant, Feta, Bulgur, and Chickpea Salad (page 67); or **Mediterranean Harvest Bowl** (recipe follows)

Dinner: 3-ounce serving of pork tenderloin, beef sirloin, or roast chicken served with **French Potato Salad** (recipe follows) and a mixed greens salad with Honey-Mustard Vinaigrette (page 86)

Dessert: 2 fresh figs

MEDITERRANEAN HARVEST BOWL (SERVES 2)

Swap out the vegetables depending on the season. In the summer months, try tomatoes, corn, and zucchini instead of sweet potato, Brussels sprouts, and cranberries. This hearty bowl also tastes great with wild rice instead of bulgur.

- **¼ cup bulgur**
- **1 sweet potato, chopped**
- **½ pound Brussels sprouts, halved**
- **1 tablespoon olive oil**
- **¼ cup almonds**
- **2 ounces Gorgonzola cheese**
- **¼ cup dried cranberries**
- **Salt and pepper, to taste**

Cook bulgur according to package instructions. Preheat oven to 400°F and line a baking sheet with aluminum foil.

Toss sweet potato and Brussels sprouts in a medium bowl with olive oil. Spread evenly on baking sheet. Roast for 20-25 minutes, until vegetables are fork-tender.

Evenly divide bulgur and vegetable mix into two bowls. Top each evenly with almonds, cheese, and dried cranberries.

FRENCH POTATO SALAD (SERVES 6)

The key to this delicious salad is adding the dressing while the potatoes are still warm. Leave the potatoes unpeeled if you wish - less fuss and more fiber.

- **6-8 medium yellow potatoes**
- **2 tablespoons extra-virgin olive oil**
- **1 tablespoon Dijon mustard**
- **1 teaspoon dried tarragon**
- **Salt and pepper, to taste**

Cook potatoes in a large pot of boiling water until they can be easily pierced with a knife. Drain and let cool slightly.

Combine olive oil and mustard in small bowl. When potatoes are cool enough to handle but still warm, chop them into a large bowl. Add dressing and toss to coat. Add tarragon and season with salt and pepper. Serve warm or cold.

Breakfast: ½ cup plain Greek yogurt topped with ¼ cup granola and 1 large diced peach; or 1-2-3 breakfast of your choice (page 13)

Lunch: Leftover French Potato Salad (page 69) with 4 ounces of meat, served with a mixed greens salad with Honey-Mustard Vinaigrette (page 86); or **Citrus Salad** (recipe follows) served with 1 slice whole grain bread spread with 1 tablespoon goat cheese

Dinner: **Eggs Shakshouka** (recipe follows) served with whole grain pita or bread

Dessert: 1 cup grapes

CITRUS SALAD (SERVES 1)

For a different flavor, substitute grapefruit sections for the orange or use a few of each. You can also swap diced walnuts or almonds for the peanuts.

- **1 cup baby spinach leaves**
- **1 orange, peeled and sectioned**
- **½ avocado, cut into chunks**
- **2 slices red onion**
- **2 tablespoons peanuts, crushed**
- **1 tablespoon Lemon Vinaigrette (page 86)**

Arrange spinach on a plate or in a shallow salad bowl. Top with orange, avocado, onion, and peanuts, and drizzle on dressing.

EGGS SHAKSHOUKA (SERVES 6)

Shakshouka is a North African dish made simply by poaching eggs in spicy tomato sauce. It looks impressive for the amount of work and the low cost of the ingredients. Serve it at your next brunch or for a quick dinner.

- 1 tablespoon olive oil
- 1 small yellow onion, diced
- 1 clove garlic, minced
- 1 red bell pepper, diced
- 2 (14-ounce) cans no-salt diced tomatoes, or about 4 cups ripe diced tomatoes
- 2 tablespoons tomato paste
- ½ teaspoon mild chili powder

- 1 teaspoon cumin
- 1 teaspoon paprika
- Pinch of cayenne pepper, or more to taste
- Salt and pepper, to taste
- 6 eggs
- 1 tablespoon minced fresh parsley, for garnish

Heat olive oil in a large skillet or Dutch oven over medium-high heat. Add onion; sauté until translucent, about 5 minutes. Add garlic and sauté until fragrant, about a minute more. Add diced pepper and cook until softened, about 7-10 minutes. Add diced tomatoes, tomato paste, and spices; bring to a simmer. Add a little bit of spice at the beginning so you can adjust to your preference. Reduce heat to low and simmer for about 5 minutes, until liquid begins to reduce. Adjust the spice and other seasoning to taste.

For the eggs, create space in the sauce for each egg with a ladle or large spoon. Rest the spoon in the sauce and crack the egg open into it. Gently remove the spoon, allowing the egg to settle into the space left behind. Repeat for the remaining 5 eggs. Cover and simmer for 10-15 minutes, checking regularly, until eggs are cooked to your liking. Garnish with minced parsley and serve.

DAY 25

Breakfast: 2 slices whole grain toast spread with 2 tablespoons peanut butter or almond butter and topped with 4 sliced figs; or 1-2-3 breakfast of your choice (page 13)

Lunch: Leftover Citrus Salad (page 70) served with 1 whole grain pita; or **Moroccan Spiced Carrot Soup** (recipe follows) served with 1 whole grain roll and an arugula salad with goat cheese, walnuts, and Balsamic Vinaigrette (page 86)

Dinner: **Herb-Baked Fish** (page 53) served over **Polenta with Sundried Tomato Pesto** (recipe follows) and sautéed kale or spinach

Dessert: 1 large plum

MOROCCAN SPICED CARROT SOUP (SERVES 4)

This creamy soup recipe showcases the vibrant spices of the Mediterranean.

- 2 tablespoons olive oil
- 12 medium carrots, grated (6 cups, grated)
- 1 red onion, diced
- 1 onion, diced
- 1 cup red lentils
- ¼ teaspoon ground cumin

- ¼ teaspoon ground ginger
- ¼ teaspoon ground cinnamon
- ¼ teaspoon ground coriander
- ⅛ teaspoon ground cayenne pepper
- 4 cups low-sodium vegetable broth
- Salt and pepper, to taste

Heat olive oil in a large pot over medium heat. Add carrots and onions; cover and cook for 15 minutes, stirring occasionally. Vegetables should be tender and starting to brown.

Add red lentils. Stir in cumin, ginger, cinnamon, coriander, and cayenne pepper, and cook another 30 seconds.

Add broth, bring soup to a boil, let simmer for 2-3 minutes, then remove from heat.

Using a blender (in batches) or an immersion blender, blend the soup until smooth. Add water as necessary for desired consistency. Season with salt and pepper.

POLENTA WITH SUNDRIED TOMATO PESTO (SERVES 4)

This recipe makes about 1 cup of pesto. Reserve the extra for the Sundried Tomato Pesto and White Bean Wrap for lunch on Day 26. Or, toss with cooked whole grain pasta and chickpeas.

- **1 cup dried whole grain polenta or whole grain corn grits**
- **1 cup sundried tomatoes, drained**
- **4 garlic cloves, peeled**
- **½ cup fresh basil**
- **¼ cup walnuts**
- **1 teaspoon red pepper flakes**
- **¼ cup olive oil**

Prepare polenta on the stovetop according to package instructions.

While polenta is cooking, add all other ingredients except olive oil to a food processor or blender and pulse until well-combined. Add olive oil and continue pulsing until well mixed.

Stir ½ cup of the pesto into polenta, then divide into four bowls.

Breakfast: **Roasted Red Pepper and Avocado Tartine** (page 44) served with 1 kiwifruit; or 1-2-3 breakfast of your choice (page 13)

Lunch: Leftover Polenta with Sundried Tomato Pesto, Herb-Roasted Fish, and sautéed greens (page 73); or **Sundried Tomato Pesto and White Bean Wrap** (recipe follows)

Dinner: **Pasta with Nonna's Quick Tomato Sauce** (recipe follows) served with sautéed broccolini with lemon and garlic

Dessert: 1 pear served with 1 ounce Kasseri cheese (or other traditional, artisan cheese)

SUNDRIED TOMATO PESTO
AND WHITE BEAN WRAP (SERVES 1)

Sundried tomatoes and white beans are a match made in the Mediterranean.

- **1 whole grain pita or tortilla**
- **2 tablespoons Sundried Tomato Pesto (leftover from Day 25 dinner)**
- **⅓ cup cooked white beans (like navy or cannellini)**
- **⅓ cup arugula**

Mash white beans with a fork. Spread whole grain pita or tortilla with sundried tomato pesto, mashed white beans, and arugula. Roll into a wrap.

PASTA WITH NONNA'S QUICK TOMATO SAUCE (SERVES 4)

For a heartier spaghetti dish, we sometimes like to toss in a can of chickpeas. Think of them as tiny "meatballs."

- 8 ounces whole grain spaghetti
- 1 tablespoon olive oil
- 2 garlic cloves, minced
- 1 (28-ounce) can crushed tomatoes
- 1 teaspoon dried oregano
- 4 ounces Pecorino Romano cheese, grated
- Salt and pepper, to taste

Cook pasta according to package instructions.

Meanwhile, heat olive oil in a medium-sized pan over low-medium heat. Add garlic to pan and heat for 30 seconds. Add crushed tomatoes and oregano. Cook for 5 minutes until heated through. Season with salt and pepper.

Add cooked pasta to pan and coat with tomato sauce. Serve pasta topped with grated cheese.

Breakfast: 1 egg scrambled with ½ chopped bell pepper, 1 small chopped onion, and 1 ounce Kasseri cheese (or Provolone cheese), served with 1 whole grain pita and 1 cup blackberries; or 1-2-3 breakfast of your choice (page 13)

Lunch: Leftover Pasta with Nonna's Quick Tomato Sauce (page 75) and broccolini; or **Veggie Omelet** (recipe follows) served with 1 slice whole grain bread and ½ cup carrot sticks

Dinner: **Spaghetti Squash and Shrimp Scampi** (recipe follows) served with roasted Brussels sprouts

Dessert: 1 cup cubed cantaloupe

VEGGIE OMELET (SERVES 2)

You can also add onions, yellow squash, or leftover cooked vegetables.

- **1 tablespoon extra-virgin olive oil**
- **1 small zucchini, diced**
- **1 red or orange bell pepper, diced**

- **1 teaspoon dried tarragon**
- **2 eggs**
- **2 teaspoons water**

Heat olive oil in a small skillet over medium-low heat. Add zucchini and pepper; sauté for about 5 minutes until vegetables soften. Turn heat up to medium-high and cook for a few minutes more until the liquid in the skillet evaporates.

Combine tarragon, eggs, and water in a small bowl and beat until smooth. Pour egg mixture into the skillet on top of the vegetables, reduce heat to medium-low, and cook until the edges of the omelet are set.

Gently running a spatula under the eggs, lift up and tilt the skillet to let some of the uncooked egg run into the bottom. Continue cooking for about 3 minutes longer, until the eggs are set.

SPAGHETTI SQUASH AND SHRIMP SCAMPI (SERVES 4)

Once baked, the flesh of spaghetti squash forms tender, spaghetti-like strands, making this dish a family-friendly way to enjoy more squash.

- **1 large spaghetti squash**
- **1 onion, chopped**
- **2 tablespoons olive oil**
- **4 garlic cloves, minced**
- **½ teaspoon red pepper flakes**

- **2 tablespoon capers**
- **12 kalamata olives**
- **½ cup white wine**
- **1 pound shrimp**
- **Handful of parsley, chopped**

Preheat oven to 375°F. Place squash in a 9x13" baking dish and add 1 cup water. Bake for 35 minutes or until a fork can easily pierce through the squash skin. Wait for squash to cool, then scrape out insides to form strands.

Heat olive oil in a skillet over medium heat. Add onions and cook for 5-7 minutes, until translucent. Add garlic and red pepper flakes and cook for 1 minute. Add capers, olives, and white wine. Simmer for 2-3 minutes, stirring occasionally.

Add shrimp to skillet and simmer for 6-8 minutes, until shrimp starts to curl and becomes pink. Stir in parsley and mix well. Divide spaghetti squash into four bowls and top evenly with shrimp scampi.

Breakfast: 2 slices whole grain toast spread with ½ medium avocado and sprinkled with za'atar seasoning, served with 1 cup strawberries mixed with ½ cup plain Greek yogurt; or 1-2-3 breakfast of your choice (page 13)

Lunch: Leftover Spaghetti Squash and Shrimp Scampi (page 77) and roasted Brussels sprouts; or **Mediterranean Salad with Radishes, Chickpeas, and Farro** (recipe follows)

Dinner: **Sheet Pan Harissa Chicken with Sweet Potatoes and Leeks** (recipe follows)

Dessert: **Almond Cookie with Tahini and Honey** (page 84)

MEDITERRANEAN SALAD WITH RADISHES, CHICKPEAS, AND FARRO (SERVES 2)

In this salad, chewy grains of farro act as the "croutons."

- **⅓ cup farro**
- **3 cups fresh spinach**
- **4 radishes, thinly sliced**
- **1 (15-ounce) can chickpeas, drained and rinsed**
- **¼ cup fresh parsley, chopped**
- **1 large lemon, zested and juiced**
- **¼ cup tahini**
- **2 tablespoons water**

Cook farro according to package instructions. In a small bowl, combine lemon juice and 1 teaspoon lemon zest. Add tahini and water; mix well.

In a large bowl, combine spinach, farro, radishes, chickpeas, and parsley. Drizzle dressing over the salad and toss until well-combined.

SHEET PAN HARISSA CHICKEN WITH SWEET POTATOES AND LEEKS (SERVES 6)

The harissa has quite a kick. For a less-spicy version, you can use half the amount of harissa.

- 2 cups plain Greek yogurt, divided
- ⅓ cup harissa
- 2 pounds boneless, skinless chicken thighs
- 2½ pounds sweet potatoes, diced
- 2 leeks

- ½ teaspoon lemon zest
- ½ teaspoons salt
- 1½ tablespoons olive oil
- 1 clove garlic
- ¼ teaspoon pepper
- *Optional: Fresh herbs, for garnish (such as parsley, dill, or mint)*

Mix 1 cup yogurt with harissa in a 1-gallon zip-top bag. Add chicken and sweet potatoes; massage to coat. Press out air and seal. Refrigerate for 8-24 hours.

Preheat oven to 425°F. In a medium bowl, combine leeks, lemon zest, salt, and olive oil. Using two large baking sheets, arrange chicken and potatoes in a single layer and roast for 20 minutes. Toss potatoes, then top each baking sheet with leeks, and cook until internal temperature of chicken reaches 165°, about 25 minutes longer.

While chicken is cooking, mix 1 cup yogurt, 2 tablespoons water, ¼ teaspoon salt, and ¼ teaspoon pepper in a small bowl. Spoon the yogurt sauce over the cooked chicken and vegetables before serving, then top with fresh herbs of choice, if desired.

Congratulations on completing your 28-day journey! In these pages, we hope that you've uncovered simple, flavorful recipes that you can turn to time-and-time again. Now that you've mastered this menu plan, you might be wondering, "What's next?" Here are some helpful tips to turn your crash course in the Mediterranean Diet into a lifestyle that you can stick with for decades to come.

Meal plan. Whether you follow this 28-day menu plan or customize a menu of your own, having a weekly meal plan is helpful way to stay on track with your nutrition goals. Pick a few healthy recipes each week to build your meals around, then grocery shop with a list.

Find your meal "formulas". By now you're familiar with our "1-2-3 breakfast" approach of whole grains + fruit + protein (page 13). But this approach can also work for lunch or dinner. Try a 1-2-3 meal of whole grains + vegetables + protein. For example, a farro and kale salad with salmon, or a whole grain pasta dish with chickpeas and grilled peppers. The combinations are endless!

Stay inspired. Looking for even more Mediterranean Diet ideas? Subscribe to Fresh Fridays, Oldways' free bi-weekly email newsletter. Each issue takes a deep dive into a Mediterranean ingredient, region, or dish, and features a handful of tasty recipes. Visit **OldwaysPT.org/FreshFridays** to learn more.

We also have a wealth of other recipes on our website at: **OldwaysPT.org/recipes**

Travel with us. There's no better way to immerse yourself in the Mediterranean Diet than by experiencing it. At Oldways, we offer culinary travel programs throughout the Mediterranean, to destinations such as Greece, Italy, Spain, Cyprus, and Turkey. Visit **OldwaysPT.org/travel** to learn about our next trip.

TIPS FOR HEALTHIER EATING

Here are some easy ways to make gradual but important changes in the way you eat.

Experiment with making different types of salads. You don't need to get stuck in the lettuce-tomato-dressing rut. Fruits, beans, fish, cheeses, nuts, olives, and a variety of greens offer endless combinations.

Pick a different raw veggie each week for afternoon snacking. Enjoy carrot sticks, bell pepper strips, or cucumber slices with 1 tablespoon of hummus or nut butter.

Eat fruit as an afternoon snack, too. Fruit provides vitamins and nutrients, and satisfies the sweet tooth without the dangers of a sugar crash afterwards.

On weekends, make a pot of soup for the week ahead. Freeze into single or double serving portions, and you can grab one for a quick lunch fix or for dinner.

Keep homemade trail mix in an airtight container in the kitchen. Every week top it off, changing up the mix of nuts and dried fruits. No time for breakfast? Grab a handful. A small amount is very filling.

Use canned, rinsed beans (black, pinto, chickpeas, white). Add to pasta dishes, salsas, and salads as for an inexpensive fiber and protein boost.

Dilute fruit juice. With half sparkling water the calories are cut in half. Or, instead of drinking juice, have a piece of fruit and a glass of water.

Measure snack foods (popcorn, chips). Instead of eating directly out of the bag, pour into a bowl, especially when relaxing in the evening. Limit your snack to about 1 cup.

Drink lots of water. You've heard it a million times, but once more won't hurt. Oftentimes when we think we're hungry, we're actually slightly dehydrated.

At a restaurant, eat half (or less) of the food that's served. Take the rest home for lunch or dinner the next day. Or, share an appetizer, entrée, and dessert with your dining companion. Savor all the elements of a quality meal while keeping calories in check and eating smaller portions.

PEACH AND BLUEBERRY CROSTATA (SERVES 8)

In the spirit of the Mediterranean Diet, this recipe harnesses the natural sweetness of fruits to flavor the crostata. We used summer fruits (peaches and blueberries), but any fruit will do. The fruit is showcased in a rich 100% whole wheat pastry crust, where some of the butter is replaced with olive oil.

For the Whole Grain Crust:

- **1 cup white whole wheat flour**
- **¼ teaspoon baking powder**
- **¼ teaspoon salt**
- **3 tablespoons cold unsalted butter**
- **3 tablespoons olive oil**
- **2 tablespoons orange juice (optional)**
- **2-4 tablespoons ice water**

For the Filling:

- **1½ pounds firm, ripe peaches, sliced**
- **½ pint fresh blueberries**
- **½ teaspoon orange zest**
- **2 tablespoons orange juice**

Mix dry crust ingredients in a large bowl. Cut butter in small cubes, then work into dry ingredients using a pastry blender or a fork until the dough is crumbly and butter pieces are smaller than peas. Add olive oil. Sprinkle orange juice over the dough and mix lightly by hand. Add ice water a little at a time, mixing lightly by hand until the dough hangs together when you grab a handful.

Turn the dough out onto a well-floured board, roll it into a ball, and form a flat disk. Wrap the disks in plastic and refrigerate for at least 1 hour.

Preheat oven to 450°F. Line a baking sheet with parchment paper. Roll the pastry into an 11-inch circle on a lightly floured surface. Transfer it to the baking sheet.

Toss all filling ingredients in a large bowl until combined. Evenly sprinkle the fruit in the center of the dough. Gently fold the border of the pastry over the fruit, pleating it to make an edge.

Bake the crostata for 20 to 25 minutes, until the crust is golden and the fruit is tender. Let the crostata cool for 5 minutes, then use two large spatulas to transfer it to a wire rack. Serve warm or at room temperature.

ALMOND COOKIES WITH TAHINI AND HONEY (SERVES 12)

Tahini is the paste of ground up sesame seeds. These cookies use almonds as the base, inspired by the traditional almond cakes of Spain. Think of these as an elegant, Mediterranean version of peanut butter cookies.

- ¾ cup tahini
- ½ cup honey
- ½ teaspoon cinnamon
- ½ teaspoon ground cardamom
- ¼ teaspoon ground ginger
- ½ teaspoon baking powder
- ½ teaspoon salt
- 2 cups almond meal

Preheat oven to 350°F. In a large bowl, combine tahini and honey and stir until combined. Add cinnamon, cardamom, ginger, baking powder, and salt; continue mixing. Add almond meal and stir until well-combined.

Roll 2 tablespoons of dough into a ball in your hands, then place on a parchment-lined baking sheet and press down to flatten (they won't expand too much in the oven), making about 12 cookies.

Bake for about 16 minutes, then let cool for 10 minutes before removing from baking sheet.

WATERMELON GRANITA (SERVES 8)

Granita is a fun, refreshing treat for sunny Mediterranean days. Fruits like watermelon and lemon give this granita a natural, bright flavor.

- **2 cups water**
- **3 tablespoons sugar**
- **4 lemons, juiced**
- **½ watermelon (seeds removed, or seedless), puréed (about 4 cups)**
- **Mint leaves, for garnish**

In a small pot, boil 1 cup of water with sugar in order to dissolve it.

Place lemon juice and watermelon purée in a large, glass baking dish. Add dissolved sugar into the dish, then add remaining cup of water. Mix gently, but not in excess, and then freeze the mixture.

After 3-4 hours, or just before serving, remove the mixture from the freezer and scratch it with a fork to produce a granita-like texture. Serve by scooping into small bowls, then decorating each portion with a mint leaf.

Recipe adapted from Alessandro Luchetti.

DRESSING BASICS

SALAD DRESSING

Dressings add a lot of flavor to green, grain, and pasta salads. They can also add a lot of calories and fat, so it pays to measure what you're using. Get into the habit of making your own simple salad dressings to bring clean, sharp flavor to all kinds of salads without adding a lot of salt. Keep a container of dressing on hand for drizzling a small amount (1 tablespoon per person or less) on salads or cooked vegetables.

VINAIGRETTE *Makes ¾ cup*

- **¼ cup cider or wine vinegar**
- **½ cup extra-virgin olive oil**
- **¼ teaspoon salt**

Combine all ingredients in a jar with a tight-fitting lid and shake until well-blended, or whisk ingredients in a bowl.

VARIATIONS

Balsamic Vinaigrette

Use balsamic vinegar instead.

Herb Vinaigrette

Add 1 tablespoon fresh chopped thyme, tarragon, or rosemary to the dressing.

Lemon Vinaigrette

Add the juice of 1-2 lemons.

Honey-Mustard Vinaigrette

Add 1-2 minced garlic cloves, 1 teaspoon Dijon mustard, and 1 teaspoon honey.

AVOCADO DRESSING *Makes about 1 cup*

- ¼ cup fresh lemon or lime juice
- 1 small avocado
- 1 clove garlic, minced
- ½ cup extra-virgin olive oil
- ¼ teaspoon salt
- ¼ teaspoon pepper

Combine juice, avocado, and garlic in a food processor or blender and purée. With the machine running, slowly add the oil. Season to taste with salt and pepper.

YOGURT-HERB DRESSING *Makes about 1 cup*

- ¾ cup plain Greek yogurt
- 1 clove garlic, minced
- 1 tablespoon Dijon mustard
- 1 tablespoon fresh tarragon or 1 teaspoon dried tarragon
- ⅓ cup fresh parsley, chopped
- Salt and pepper

Combine yogurt, garlic, mustard, and herbs in a food processor or blender and purée. Season to taste with salt and pepper.

CAESAR DRESSING *Makes about ½ cup*

- 3 ounces silken tofu
- ½ lemon, juiced
- 1 tablespoon Dijon mustard
- 2 garlic cloves
- 1 teaspoon anchovy paste
- ¼ teaspoon salt
- 2 tablespoons Parmigiano-Reggiano cheese
- 1 tablespoon olive oil
- 1 tablespoon balsamic vinegar

Combine all ingredients in a food processor or blender and mix until well-combined.

A GUIDE TO WHOLE GRAINS

WHAT'S A WHOLE GRAIN?

Whole grains have three edible parts: the outer bran layers, rich in fiber and B vitamins; the germ, full of antioxidants; and the starchy endosperm.

Much of the grain kernel's nutrients—and flavor—are in the bran and germ, which are routinely stripped out to make white flour. Some grains are then enriched—but this returns only about five of the many missing nutrients.

Your best bet for good health? Look for whole grains. Even if they've been ground into flour, rolled into flakes, or mixed into pasta or bread, they're whole grains if all of the three original parts are still present in their original proportions.

FINDING WHOLE GRAINS

Mediterranean whole grains are often wheat-based, including bulgur, freekeh, farro, spelt, whole wheat couscous, and whole wheat breads and pastas. Barley and rice are also easy to find throughout the Mediterranean. Look for products that display the Whole Grain Stamp (left), which tells you how much whole grain is in a serving.

To learn more about whole grains, visit www.WholeGrainsCouncil.org.

TIME-SAVING TIPS

While it's not too hard to get water going for a pot of quicker-cooking whole grains, it's even easier on a busy night to simply reheat what's waiting for you, cooked, in the refrigerator or freezer. Try cooking grains on the weekend when you're doing something else in the kitchen. Store leftovers in the refrigerator for up to five days, or freeze portions in zip-lock bags. Just reheat them in the microwave or toss by the handful into stews and soups.

TRADITIONAL MEDITERRANEAN GRAINS

A rich, golden, corn polenta. Whole wheat couscous. Bulgur mixed with cucumbers, tomatoes, mint, and parsley to make tabbouleh. A savory risotto. Traditional Mediterranean dishes offer a wide variety of options for enjoying more whole grains.

Barley: Look for hulled or hull-less barley; pearled barley is not a whole grain. Add barley to vegetable soups and stews, or combine with cucumbers, onions, and feta for a grain salad. Many people also make barley "risotto."

Bulgur: Bulgur can be finely-ground or coarse. Coarse bulgur may need to be simmered for 5 minutes and then left covered for 20 minutes or so to absorb its liquid. Fine bulgur can be simply added to boiling water or broth, then left covered for 20 minutes or more while you cook the rest of your meal. Use it to make **Tabbouleh** (page 52); mix with walnuts and lemon juice to stuff peppers; or simply enjoy it as a side dish instead of rice.

Brown Rice: Use long grain for pilafs and short grain for creamy risottos. Look for red rice, black rice, and other colors that are also whole grain!

Couscous: Couscous is not a grain (there are no couscous plants!), but instead is a small pasta-like granule made from either refined wheat or whole wheat. Be sure to look for the whole wheat kind. Serve with stews or North African curries.

Farro: Farro is a kind of wheat traditional to Italy. Look for whole farro (not pearled, or "semi-perlato"). Use it in salads, stews, or side dishes.

GRAIN COOKING CHART

Cooking grains is easy. Just add your dry grain and liquid to a pot, bring to a boil, then simmer gently according to the guidelines below.

Grains vary widely in cooking time depending on the age of the grain, the variety, and the pot you're using to cook them. When you decide they're tender and tasty, they're done! If the grain is not as tender as you like when "time is up," simply add more water and continue cooking. Or, if everything seems fine before the liquid is all absorbed, simply drain the excess. Check packages for exact instructions.

1 CUP DRY GRAIN +	LIQUID	COOK TIME	COOKED GRAIN
Amaranth	2 cups	20-25 minutes	3½ cups
Barley, hulled	3 cups	45-60 minutes	3½ cups
Buckwheat	2 cups	20 minutes	4 cups
Bulgur	2 cups	5-10 minutes	3 cups
Cornmeal (polenta)	4 cups	20-30 minutes	4 cups
Couscous, whole wheat	2 cups	Let sit 15 minutes off heat after boiling	3 cups
Farro	2½ cups	25-40 minutes	3 cups
Kamut® Wheat	4 cups	45-60 minutes*	3 cups

soak overnight in liquid before cooking

1 CUP DRY GRAIN +	LIQUID	COOK TIME	COOKED GRAIN
Millet, hulled	2½ cups	25-35 minutes	4 cups
Oats, steel cut	4 cups	20 minutes	4 cups
Pasta, whole wheat	6 cups	8-12 minutes (varies by size)	Varies
Quinoa	2 cups	12-15 minutes	3+ cups
Rice, brown	2½ cups	25-45 minutes (varies by variety)	3-4 cups
Rye Berries	4 cups	45-60 minutes*	3 cups
Sorghum	4 cups	25-40 minutes	3 cups
Spelt Berries	4 cups	45-60 minutes*	3 cups
Teff	3-4 cups	15-20 minutes	3 cups
Wheat Berries	4 cups	45-60 minutes*	3 cups
Wild Rice	3 cups	45-55 minutes	3½ cups

*soak overnight in
liquid before cooking*

SNACKS AT A GLANCE

Reach for one of these snacks, or a combination of several, if you want to expand your daily calorie intake. Add one of these foods to the daily menus as an afternoon pick-me-up, and/or as a dessert for lunch or dinner.

Note: The totals below reflect estimates. Check the specific nutrition labels on any products you purchase.

	Serving Size	Calories	Fat (g)	Sat Fat (g)	Sodium (mg)	Carbs (g)	Fiber (g)	Protein (g)
Almonds	1 ounce (¼ cup)	160	14	1	0	5	3	6
Apple	1 medium	80	0	0	0	21	4	0
Baba Ghanoush	1 tablespoon	20	1	0	25	2	1	1
Bean Dip	2 tablespoons	50	2.5	0	55	6	1	1
Biscotti	1 medium	100	5	1	50	11	2	6
Cantaloupe	1 cup	60	0	0	15	13	1	1
Cheese (Brie)	1 ounce	95	8	5	120	0	0	6
Cheese (feta)	1 ounce	75	6	4	310	1	0	4
Cottage Cheese	½ cup	80	1	1	460	3	0	14
Carrots (baby)	6	25	1	0	50	6	0	0
Cashews (raw)	1 ounce (¼ cup)	160	12	2	90	9	1	5
Cherries	1 cup	90	0	0	5	19	3	1
Chocolate (dark)	1 ounce	140	10	4	30	15	1	2
Cookies (oatmeal raisin)	2	210	7	2	200	20	2	3
Crackers (whole grain)	3	60	2	1	90	9	2	2

	Serving Size	Calories	Fat (g)	Sat Fat (g)	Sodium (mg)	Carbs (g)	Fiber (g)	Protein (g)
Dates	4	90	0	0	0	25	3	1
Figs (fresh)	2	70	0	0	0	19	3	1
Gelato (vanilla)	½ cup	140	9	5	40	10	0	3
Grapes	1 cup	100	0	0	0	25	1	1
Hummus (average)	1 tablespoon	25	1	0	55	2	1	1
Latte (with 1% milk)	1 cup	110	2	2	105	12	0	8
Mango	1 cup	110	0	0	0	28	3	1
Olives (Kalamata)	6	40	3	0	220	3	1	0
Orange	1 medium	60	0	0	0	14	3	1
Peanuts (roasted, unsalted)	1 ounce (¼ cup)	160	14	3	0	6	3	9
Peanut Butter (smooth, unsalted)	1 tablespoon	90	8	1	60	3	1	4
Pita (whole grain)	1 small	70	1	0	150	15	2	3
Pistachios	1 ounce (¼ cup)	150	12	2	0	8	3	6
Popcorn (unbuttered)	2 cups	60	0	0	0	12	2	2
Sorbet (raspberry)	½ cup	100	0	0	0	15	1	0
Sunflower Seeds (hulled, roasted, without salt)	1 ounce (¼ cup)	160	14	2	0	7	3	6
Trail Mix (average)	¼ cup	170	11	2	85	17	2	6
Yogurt, Greek (2%)	6 ounces	130	3.5	2	70	7	0	17
Walnuts	1 ounce (¼ cup)	190	18	2	0	4	2	4

RECIPE INDEX AND NUTRITIONALS

Page		Calories	Fat (g)	Sat Fat (g)	Sodium (mg)	Carbs (g)	Fiber (g)	Protein (g)
Fish and Seafood								
53	Herb-Baked Fish	210	8	2	200	0	0	33
47	Lemon and Caper Cod with Potatoes	300	12	1.5	390	24	4	28
39	Mussels Provençal	140	2	0.5	170	9	1	11
20	Salmon Salad Sandwich	300	4	0	490	43	7	28
63	Sardine Puttanesca	320	9	1	170	44	6	17
35	Six-Minute Shrimp with Whole Grain Linguine	200	9	1	170	5	1	24
60	Smoked Salmon Sandwich	460	19	3.5	290	32	5	43
77	Spaghetti Squash and Shrimp Scampi	290	11	2	550	17	3	28
19	Spicy Salmon	270	12	2	330	2	1	17
Poultry								
37	Chicken Kebabs with Yogurt Sauce	160	1.5	0	95	4	0	32
43	Chicken with Romesco Sauce	380	21	3	140	6	2	41
31	Pasta with Chicken Sausage and Roasted Broccoli	460	13	2	420	61	8	30
59	Rosemary Roasted Chicken	320	14	2.5	170	0	0	47
79	Sheet Pan Harissa Chicken with Sweet Potatoes and Leeks	450	12	3	540	46	6	37
Meat								
27	Vegetable-Beef Kebabs	190	8	2.5	40	11	3	20
Meatless								
25	Artichoke and Spinach Frittata	230	14	6	490	6	1	19
29	Cauliflower with Chickpeas	260	9	1	590	40	10	9
71	Eggs Shakshouka	140	7	2	100	10	2	8

Page		Calories	Fat (g)	Sat Fat (g)	Sodium (mg)	Carbs (g)	Fiber (g)	Protein (g)
Meatless (cont.)								
56	Fig and Manchego Sandwich	380	12	0.5	480	53	4	14
54	Hummus and Garden Veggie Sandwich	340	16	6	590	33	3	17
68	Mediterranean Harvest Bowl	400	22	7	410	44	12	16
26	Meze Plate	220	8	3	410	27	4	10
28	Meze Rollup	320	14	2.5	590	42	1	11
75	Pasta with Nonna's Quick Tomato Sauce	290	8	3.5	480	39	8	15
55	Pasta with Fresh Tomatoes and Basil	400	16	6	360	49	7	20
22	Pesto, Mozzarella, Tomato, and Arugula Sandwich	400	25	6	590	30	5	17
41	Polenta with Greens and Fried Eggs	350	17	5	470	30	3	19
73	Polenta with Sundried Tomato Pesto	230	12	1.5	45	27	6	3
45	Roasted Butternut Squash Pasta	465	21	6.5	410	59	10	19
61	Roasted Cauliflower Pasta	470	21	6	390	52	9	21
44	Roasted Red Pepper and Avocado Tartine	430	18	3	430	53	7	8
46	Spanish Picnic	390	33	7	420	36	5	16
51	Spinach-Mushroom Strata	340	17	7	430	30	4	18
74	Sundried Tomato Pesto and White Bean Wrap	350	12	1.5	480	53	8	14
66	Tomato Basil Quinoa	400	14	6	720	47	8	22
76	Veggie Omelet	150	12	2.5	75	4	2	7
21	Whole Grain Spaghetti with Arugula Walnut Pesto	450	22	2	330	49	8	16

RECIPE INDEX AND NUTRITIONALS

Page		Calories	Fat (g)	Sat Fat (g)	Sodium (mg)	Carbs (g)	Fiber (g)	Protein (g)
	Soups							
36	Hearty Tomato Soup with Citrus Cod	330	5	1	590	35	13	34
23	Lentil Soup	210	10	3	270	21	5	9
30	Minestrone	260	6	1	300	41	9	10
72	Moroccan Spiced Carrot Soup	340	7	1	270	53	9	15
42	Roasted Butternut Squash Soup	165	4	0.5	290	34	6	3
58	Roasted Cauliflower Soup	110	7	1	330	10	4	4
	Salads							
62	Chicken Caesar Salad	360	15	3	520	5	1	54
38	Chickpea Salad	140	2	0	220	23	6	9
70	Citrus Salad	420	34	3	85	30	8	8
67	Eggplant, Feta, Bulgur, and Chickpea Salad	420	22	5	300	49	15	14
40	Fattoush	250	13	4	400	31	7	9
34	Fennel, Orange, and Beet Salad	450	25	6	600	50	14	14
69	French Potato Salad	230	5	1	75	44	5	5
50	Massaged Kale Salad with Farro and Sweet Potato	430	22	3.5	520	48	11	14
24	Mediterranean Orzo Salad	460	13	4	340	74	14	19
78	Mediterranean Salad with Radishes, Chickpeas, and Farro	470	19	2.5	350	61	13	20
18	Simple Bistro Salad	280	14.5	3	310	22	7	14
52	Tabbouleh	140	1	0	55	30	10	6
57	Whole Grain Panzanella Salad with Tomatoes and Olives	420	22	3	470	42	5	16

Page		Calories	Fat (g)	Sat Fat (g)	Sodium (mg)	Carbs (g)	Fiber (g)	Protein (g)
Dips, Dressings, and Spreads								
87	Avocado Dressing	70	8	1	40	1	1	0
86	Balsamic Vinaigrette	80	9	1	50	1	0	0
87	Caesar Dressing	80	8	1.5	340	3	0	4
86	Herb Vinaigrette	80	9	1	50	1	0	0
86	Honey-Mustard Vinaigrette	80	9	1	60	1	0	0
86	Lemon Vinaigrette	80	9	1	50	1	0	0
87	Yogurt-Herb Dressing	15	0	0	55	1	0	2
Desserts								
84	Almond Cookies with Tahini and Honey	240	17	2	130	19	3	7
82	Peach and Blueberry Crostata	180	10	3.5	90	23	3	3
85	Watermelon Granita	110	0	0	0	28	1	2

INDEX

A
Apple 13, 42, 43, 50, 92
Arugula 12, 21, 22, 56, 60, 74
Avocado 13, 34, 44, 54, 60, 70, 87

B
Basil 24, 55, 57, 66, 73
Beans 12, 21, 30, 55, 66, 74
Beef 27
Broccoli 31
Bulgur 52, 67, 68, 89, 90

C
Capers 47, 63, 77
Carrot 18, 30, 46, 72, 92
Cauliflower 29, 58, 61
Cheese
  Feta 12, 23, 24, 28, 34, 40, 50, 67, 92
  Fontina Val d'Aosta 51
  Gorgonzola 45, 68
  Kasseri 12, 54
  Manchego 12, 46, 56
  Mozzarella 22
  Parmigiano-Reggiano 12, 53, 87
  Pecorino Romano 12, 25, 41, 55, 61, 66, 75
Chicken 37, 43, 59, 62, 79
  Sausage 31, 57
Chickpeas 24, 29, 34, 38, 50, 67, 78
Couscous 38, 89, 90
Crostata 82
Cucumber 18, 34, 38, 40

E
Eggplant 24, 67
Eggs 13, 18, 25, 41, 51, 71, 76

F
Farro 50, 78, 89, 90
Fattoush 40
Fig 13, 56, 93
Fish, Seafood
  Anchovy Paste 87
  Cod 36, 47
  Herb-Baked 53
  Mussels 39
  Salmon 19, 20, 60
  Sardines 63
  Shrimp 35, 77
Frittata 25

G
Granita 85

H
Harissa 79
Hummus 13, 26, 28, 54, 93

K
Kale 50
Kebab, Beef 27
Kebab, Chicken 37

L
Leek 79
Lemon 18, 19, 20, 23, 24, 27, 37, 40, 47, 50, 52, 59, 60, 67, 78, 79, 85, 86, 87
Lentil 12, 23

M
Meze
  Plate 15, 26
  Rollup 28
Mint 52, 67, 85
Mushroom 27, 51
Mustard, Dijon 51, 69, 86, 87

N
Nut
  Almond 43, 46, 50, 68, 84, 92
  Peanut 70, 93
  Pecan 34
  Pine 67
  Pistachio 93
  Walnut 21, 22, 28, 45, 61, 73, 93

O
Oatmeal 34
Olives 12, 26, 57, 77, 93
Orange 13, 34, 36, 70, 82, 93

P
Panzanella 57
Parsley 40, 43, 45, 52, 61, 63, 67, 71, 77, 78, 87

Pasta
    Mediterranean Orzo Salad 24
    Mussels Provençal 39
    Roasted Butternut Squash 45
    Roasted Cauliflower 61
    Sardine Puttanesca 63
    Six-Minute Shrimp 35
    with Arugula Walnut Pesto 21
    with Chicken Sausage and Roasted Broccoli 31
    with Fresh Tomatoes and Basil 55
    with Nonna's Quick Tomato Sauce 75
Pepper, Bell 24, 27, 29, 40, 57, 71, 76
Pepper, Roasted 28, 43, 44
Pesto
    Arugula Walnut 21, 22
    Sundried Tomato 73, 74
Polenta 41, 73, 90
Potato 30, 47, 69
Potato, Sweet 50, 68, 79

Q
Quinoa 66, 91

R
Radish 18, 40, 46, 78
Rice, Brown 89, 91

S
Salad 14
    Chicken Caesar 62
    Chickpea 38
    Citrus 70
    Fattoush 40
    Fennel, Orange, and Beet 34
    French Potato 69
    Massaged Kale with Farro and Sweet Potato 50
    Mediterranean 78
    Mediterranean Orzo 24
    Simple Bistro 18
Salad Dressing 86, 87
Sandwich
    Fig and Manchego 56
    Hummus and Garden Veggie 54
    Pesto, Mozzarella, Tomato, and Arugula 22
    Roasted Red Pepper and Avocado Tartine 44

Salmon Salad 20
Smoked Salmon 60
Sauce
    Quick Tomato 75
    Romesco 43, 46
    Yogurt 37, 38
Shakshouka 71
Soup 15
    Hearty Tomato, with Citrus Cod 36
    Lentil 23
    Minestrone 30
    Moroccan Spiced Carrot 72
    Roasted Butternut Squash 42
    Roasted Cauliflower 58
Spinach 12, 14, 25, 28, 30, 51, 54, 70, 78
Squash, Butternut 12, 42, 45
Squash, Spaghetti 77
Squash, Yellow 29
Strata 51
Swiss Chard 41, 66

T
Tabbouleh 26, 52
Tahini 34, 78, 84
Tomato, Canned 23, 29, 30, 36, 43, 63, 66, 71, 75
Tomato, Fresh 18, 22, 24, 27, 38, 39, 40, 52, 55, 57, 66, 71
Tomato, Sundried 31, 73, 74

V
Vinaigrette 86

W
Watermelon 85
Whole Grain 11, 13, 14, 88, 90, 91
Wine 11, 39, 77
Wrap 14
    Meze 28
    Sundried Tomato Pesto and White Bean 74

Y
Yogurt 13, 20, 44, 79, 87, 93
    Sauce 37, 38

Z
Zucchini 12, 67, 76

rediscover goodness
OLDWAYS
CULTURAL FOOD TRADITIONS

If you enjoyed the Oldways 4-Week Mediterranean Diet Menu Plan, discover more helpful books and resources at OldwaysPT.org, including:

12 Ways To Use Vegetables

Build on what you've learned about the Mediterranean Diet and try all sorts of new ideas to enjoy vegetables in your home-cooked breakfasts, lunches, dinners, and snacks.

Oldways 4-Week Vegetarian & Vegan Diet Menu Plan

Create delicious, balanced, budget-friendly plant-based meals, and find out just how easy and satisfying going vegetarian (or vegan) can be.

Whole Grains Around the World

With inspiration from cultures around the globe, this 4-week menu plan will introduce you to many healthy and flavorful whole grains like bulgur, freekeh, farro, and more.

For these and other resources, visit OldwaysPT.org

Made in the USA
Columbia, SC
27 August 2019